I0698560

Authenticity in Leadership

Strategies to Make a Lasting Impact Amidst Complexity and Uncertainty

Josh Macalinao

Copyright © 2024 by Josh Macalinao

This document contains opinions and ideas of the authors. It is sold for the purpose of providing helpful and reliable information; the publisher, authors, and all other parties involved in the making of this document are not required to render any qualified services or advice.

The information provided herein is strictly for educational and entertainment purposes; any liability, in terms of inattention or otherwise, by any usage or abuse of any policies, processes, or directions contained within, is the solitary and utter responsibility of the reader.

The content and information contained in this book has been compiled from sources deemed reliable, and it is accurate to the best of the Author's knowledge, information and belief. However, the Author cannot guarantee its accuracy and validity and cannot be held liable for any errors and/or omissions. Further, changes are periodically made to this book as and when needed. Where appropriate and/or necessary, you must consult a professional (including but not limited to your doctor, attorney, financial advisor or such other professional advisor) before using any of the suggested remedies, techniques, or information in this book.

Under no circumstances will any legal responsibility or blame be held against the publisher, author, or any other parties involved in the making of this document for any reparation, damages, or monetary loss due to the information herein, either directly or indirectly. This disclaimer applies to any loss, damages or injury caused by the use and application, whether directly or indirectly, of any advice or information presented, whether for breach of contract, tort, negligence, personal injury, criminal intent, or under any other cause of action.

You agree to accept all risks of using the information presented inside this book.

Permission is not granted to reproduce, duplicate, or transmit any part of this document in electronic or printed format. Recording of this publication is also prohibited and storage of this document is not allowed without the written permission from the publisher.

Cover Image: This cover has been designed using assets from Freepik

All rights are reserved.

Contents

Introduction

Leadership presents a lifelong voyage filled with storms and sun-kissed horizons for those willing to chart their course. Master captains rely not on combatting winds but tacking strategically amid turbulence toward their truth north. Defining your destination requires clarifying purpose first - what legacy will you imprint on the hearts and structures influencing? Techqnical skills enable transitory effectiveness, but navigating uncharted waters demands grounding leadership in resilience and integrity.

The mythic ideal of the stoic, self-sufficient leader pushing relentlessly forward while remaining untouched by external pressures is untenable in our intricately interconnected world. Neither individuals nor organizations thrive through continual expenditure without restoration. Rather, the path to sustainable success weaves between intense effort during demand surges and intentional recovery integrating lessons.

Cultivating resilience relies on a growth mindset that frames storms as opportunities to expand capabilities rather than crises eliciting panic. With foundations anchored in integrity and purpose, leaders can respond with agility to shifts while empowering teams to channel their best selves despite uncertainty. However, personalized definitions of leadership excellence all chart different nuanced courses across contexts.

Finding Your Truth North

Voyages last beyond single careers or lifetimes — leadership lives on through talent developed, cultures transformed and communities impacted. Understanding this broader context and imprint helps leaders progress from clinging onto power towards empowering endless ripples. But vision requires navigation tools; floating adrift leaves little recordable legacy.

With so many theories flooding discourse, determining appropriate models feels akin to assembling a puzzle with pieces randomly plucked across decades. However, common threads emerge around self-awareness, adaptability, ethical grounding and nurturing talent as navigational essentials. Tracking your truth north relies on continually realigning elements as landscapes morph.

Leadership forms an inward expedition before manifesting externally. Seizing authority requires addressing fears and false narratives restricting authenticity. Mustering courage to stand firmly yet compassionately for personal truths and shared values paves pathways enabling forward movement. With your inner compass aligned, it becomes possible to chart courses empowering people over roles.

Mastering Fluidity and Flexibility

Meanwhile the terrain itself shifts continuously — economically, politically, technologically and generationally. Navigating unmapped waters demands flexibility in reinventing skillsets, mindsets and communication styles to resonate across diverse stakeholders. Attuning to undercurrents allows intentionally upskilling into emerging competencies primed for contemporary challenges.

Agility relies on embracing complexity rather than seeking simplistic explanations. The interplay between known knowns, known unknowns and unknown unknowns that characterize business volatility can trigger those without resilience. However, learning to lean into ambiguity liberates innovation from narrowly defined lanes. By expanding perspective and capabilities while demonstrating integrity, leaders fluidly pivot into newly emerging roles.

Accepting impermanence of static destinations enables appreciating daily progress on the open sea. Attachment to rigid expectations of achievement often restricts adaptability needed to redirect when volatility strikes. However, leaders focused on compounding incremental gains through new capabilities application generate momentum for talent and organizations to flow optimally.

Anchoring in Integrity

True north holds firm regardless of passing lateral waves. While technical aptitude and fluidity provide vehicles for transitory effectiveness, anchoring leadership in integrity establishes cultural cornerstones outlasting any individual tenure.

What separates resonant leaders from transient talking heads is walking espoused values within lived actions. Credibility necessitates embodying virtues across structures, processes and behaviors through transparency, psychological safety, dignity and caring. Moral foundations steer courses sustaining people's best selves and organizational potential through storms.

Navigating complex dilemmas requires examining root motivations and character beyond rule-based compliance. While legal guardrails establish ethical baselines, transcendent leadership summons moral peaks honoring humanistic values. Translating aspirational words into aligned behavior relies on shared vigilance across hierarchies to uphold standards daily.

Fostering understanding requires ongoing multidirectional dialogues challenging assumptions and locating integration opportunities when principles conflict. Hypocrisy and double standards rapidly corrode integrity. Leaders must self-reflect on how actions and incentives strengthen or undermine publicly championed values. ethics live through modeling, not mandates.

Empowering Future Generations

The enterprise must outlive any single leader's tenure. Beyond knowledge transfer lies a deeper legacy — imprinting timeless values through mentoring emerging generations. Such cultivation relies on igniting dormant embers inside rather than imposing expectations externally.

Effective succession planning prepares leaders for continuity across chapters while liberating veteran stewards to mentor proteges without becoming indispensable. Thoughtful transitions distribute wisdom across rising talent ready to chart new trajectories aligned to their strengths and passions. Release attachments to replicating your path; instead facilitate diverse thinkers pioneering new channels aligned to their truth north.

Leadership leaps from individual grasp as you tactfully transfer authority to empower broader human potential. Your voyage culminates when crews sail ahead guided by values you embedded but paths you never envisioned. In the end, captains turn the wheel over to able navigators ready to take on the watch with their own compasses in hand. Turn the page and let's start your journey!

Chapter One

Your Leadership Journey

The path to leadership is often filled with twists and turns, requiring resilience to navigate successfully. While raw talent provides a foundation, experience molds aspiring leaders through trial and error. Technical expertise alone fails to guarantee effective leadership, which hinges on the ability to motivate teams and implement strategic objectives. As such, resilience emerges as a vital attribute for overcoming obstacles and learning from failures during the leadership journey.

This chapter examines strategies to build career resilience for leadership roles. We will explore the limitations of academic and vocational training, analyze essential people skills, and provide practical steps to hone real-world leadership capabilities. By understanding the unique demands of guiding an organization, rising professionals can tailor their development toward roles of increasing responsibility. The aim is to empower both emerging and established leaders with adaptable mindsets and skill sets to thrive in dynamic work environments.

The Leadership Skills Gap

Conventional education channels often fall short in preparing future leaders. While schools and universities focus heavily on individual achievement in largely solitary endeavors, leadership requires collaboration, communication, and people management capabilities. Even subjects like business administration tend to concentrate more on operational expertise as opposed to the interpersonal aptitude modern leadership demands.

Once in the working world, professionals typically start by building technical prowess in a particular field – be it accounting, law, finance, or other realms. However, clinging too tightly to specialized skills can restrict upward mobility into enterprise leadership. After all, effective directives require strategic perspective beyond any single function. As organizations and markets continuously evolve, an obsessive focus on technical mastery breeds complacency rather than resilient thinking.

The key is to balance functional credentials with versatility cultivated through diverse experiences. For example, professionals with P&L ownership gain an enterprise orientation, understanding how decisions permeate across departments. Likewise, managing programs with cross-functional team members or rotating through different business units expands thinking beyond narrow perspectives. Such varied roles build critical thinking, adaptability, and empathy – preparing leaders to address multifaceted business challenges.

Cultivating People Skills

Interpersonal capabilities represent essential tools for resilient leaders. Unlike technical skills, people skills broadly apply across roles and industries. While certain niches like the armed forces, restaurants, and hotels hone these talents early through baptism-by-fire experiences, other professionals must intentionally foster them.

Communication stands at the heart of leadership, requiring clarity when issuing directives along with active listening and interpretation skills. Beyond information flow, leaders must master the arts of motivation and influence to propel teams toward shared objectives. This means appealing to both hearts and minds by connecting organizational goals to individual aspirations.

Leadership also involves resolving conflict, promoting collaboration, and molding team culture, requiring both empathy and assertiveness. Furthermore, strategies like delegation and change management depend upon secure relationships and psychological safety. During setbacks, resilient leaders draw upon emotional intelligence to rally collective commitment behind renewed visions.

Charting Your Leadership Path

Leadership careers rarely follow straightforward trajectories. Rather than well-defined roadmaps, professionals face winding detours and unexpected forks that test resilience. Still, while each journey is unique, common strategies exist to guide development. By balancing technical expertise with essential people skills, individuals at any career stage can mould behaviors expected of directors who motivate teams toward shared success.

Leadership Takes Shape at All Levels

A prevalent misconception holds that leadership solely resides in the C-suite. However, respondents across sectors agree director-level capabilities manifest at every tier. While early leadership may seem trivial – focused on diligence and reliability – these behaviors set the stage foradded responsibilities. The key is recognizing the next development level and adjusting approaches before transitioning up the ladder.

As professionals assume more senior positions, expectations shift from task-oriented reliability toward strategic orientation, communication savvy, and team inspiration. Those who fail to adapt often succumb to "altitude sickness" as the expectations of leadership catch them underprepared. However, by understanding differences in success criteria across career stages, individuals can intentionally hone necessary skills well in advance to smooth role transitions.

While technical expertise remains important, people management capabilities grow increasingly vital with seniority. In fact, research suggests only around a third of professionals consider top leaders effective at motivation – a severe shortcoming. Clearly, while technical qualifications open early career doors, people-centered techniques sustain enduring success in the C-suite.

Developing a Leadership Mindset

Certain beliefs represent precursors to fruitful leadership development. First, directors do not need to be superhuman; demonstrating basic diligence already exceeds common pitfalls of complacency that derail rising professionals. Additionally, leadership takes shape at all levels, not just for CEOs. By practising essential techniques early and often, skills compound over time through role progression.

With a leadership growth mentality, individuals should focus efforts on the three skill areas that display the largest gaps at respective career levels. For early tenure professionals, this means doubling down on foundational conduct like drive, dependability, and ownership. At mid-level transition points, coaching and mentoring abilities allow managers to motivate teams while ascending rungs. Finally, big picture orientation becomes critical to lead across functions, along with change management dexterity and strategic communication talents targeted toward senior leadership.

While every leadership journey follows distinctive contours, realizing development as a continuous, adaptive process allows professionals to actively shape satisfying careers. By identifying current gaps and refining abilities long before next-level demands arise, individuals build resilience to navigate leadership's twists and turns.

> Remember, leadership misconceptions that abilities spontaneously materialize or remain exclusive to the boardroom can discourage professionals from pursuing senior roles.

However, research confirms cultivating strategic, team-focused skills at progressive career tiers enables growth into directors. While early leadership centers on work ethic and reliability, managing collaboration and inspiration become increasing priorities at later stages. By balancing technical expertise with people capabilities – and understanding key transitions between levels – any professional can chart a course toward enterprise impact.

Identifying Your Leadership Style

Myriad labels exist for categorizing leadership styles exhibited by leaders. A sample of predominant styles of leadership includes:

The Coach: Focused on nurturing talent through personalized guidance on skill building to reach professional and organizational aims. They lead through serving individual growth needs.

The Visionary: Driven by a defined future vision for the organization and dedicated to rallying teams behind turning that vision into reality. They lead by illuminating the horizons ahead.

The Servant: Committed foremost to enriching institutional culture and satisfying personnel needs to indirectly achieve corporate outcomes. They lead by providing for those they oversee.

The Autocrat: Maintains strict control over processes, decisions and the direction of subordinates through formal authority rather than collective input. They lead via top-down mandate.

The savviest leaders thereby master moving strategically along a spectrum spanning structure and nurture. They uphold efficient systems while occasionally spotlighting individual welfare to lubricate institutional machinery with care. Through this fine balance, they adapt oversight styles effortlessly as scene, stakeholders and challenges shift, without allegiance to any one approach alone. But blending styles creatively rests on first grasping when visionary inspiration, democratic discussion or top-down authority best serve organizations. This contextual clarity allows proactive pivoting between directives to guide groups fluidly ahead.

So let's start building your adaptive leadership dashboard! We'll log observed scenarios, stakeholder mindsets and potential friction points within typical situations at your office. This data will reveal which leadership dials to tune for optimal outcomes as settings change.

How Leadership Style Drives Team Behaviors

A leader's communication approach sets the tone for how teams operate. Certain styles like visionary leadership spark motivation, while other personas encourage innovation or compliance. It's important that teams understand which behaviors are valued based on the leader's guiding personality.

Styles that inspire tend to boost involvement and effort from employees. Meanwhile, stricter styles raise adherence to rules. For best results, pick a style that aligns with the actions wanted. When expectations are clearly presented, teams know how to perform at their best.

Visionary Style Drives Inspired Effort

By boldly casting an ambitious vision, visionary leaders prompt team investment in realizing that future. People stretch their efforts and take risks once compelled by a motivating goal. Use this style to spur progress rapid progress towards a defined destination.

Coaching Style Drives Skill Growth

Coaches personalize guidance to each individual, helping them overcome limitations through tailored training. This nurturing drives self-improvement efforts across teams as people work to hit their potential. Use coaching to level up personnel capabilities.

Autocratic Style Drives Strict Alignment

Autocrats mandate work to be done in a top-down fashion with little input from others. This forces diligent on-plan execution yet restricts ingenuity. Use this style only when adherence matters more than problem solving.

Laissez-Faire Style Drives Bottom-Up Solutions

By granting teams freedom, laissez-faire leaders let innovative ideas and processes bubble up from the bottom. People feel activated to create better ways forward themselves. Use this style of leadership when you need emergent solutions.

If the leader's style and desired behaviors are mismatched, it leaves staff unsure how to carry out their work. This harms productivity and engagement. To avoid mixed signals, leaders must directly request the specific actions wanted. For example, when innovation is a goal, ask teams to submit all creative expansion plans.

Rather than leaving conduct open to interpretation based on personality, define precisely what is expected through both communication approach and words. Direct teams to "focus energy on securing this quarter's client wins" or to "share candidly how collaboration can improve." Clear directives empower employees to contribute meaningfully without guesswork.

Optimal results stem from sending unified messages about values and vision through an aligned leadership style and explicit requests. This removes ambiguity so teams can confidently engage and perform at their peak.

How to Develop Your Leadership Style

Leadership materializes through communication. Yet many mute their true voices attempting to match some ideal they've had in their head. This section charts a pathway to revealing your distinct leadership style voice through concrete self-examination. Learn to project honestly versus merely reflecting other figures of leadership.

Looking Inward to Lead Outward

An instinct exists to mimic perceived leadership stereotypes seen in media when first leading teams. The impulse blinds you to strengths that are making you impactful already. Avoid tropes and such trappings by ignoring outside "shoulds" as your guide.

Leadership communication flows from inner truth then resonates outward. Examples set by icons like Jobs and Sandberg, while useful to study, cannot define your personal executive presence. Let go of these limited prototypes. Your existing qualities fueled your rise already. Now build on that foundation.

Start by taking stock of communication strengths coming naturally. Are you uplifting? Detail-driven? What verbal or nonverbal tendencies engage others? Then identity slippery areas needing reinforcement through conscious effort.

Owning current abilities and challenges beats living as a weak imitation of some mythical leader. Set an intent to lead from the inside out by maximizing innate talents while refining rougher edges. Comparing yourself to just you frees discovering communication that convinces.

Harnessing Your Strengths, Developing Your Gaps

Now examine precisely how your inborn gifts equip you to guide teams. If highly collaborative, how can that talent for bridging divisions manifest through speech, gestures and choices? Then scrutinize areas needing improvement if hoping to inspire at scale.

For instance, introverts ranking low in sociability might focus on projecting assuredness when addressing crowds. They could embrace public speaking coaches to seem confident beyond feeling such. Extroverts often overflowing with passion might learn adding structure to better streamline vision sharing.

This balancing act molds well-rounded leadership presence. Shore up soft spots not to eternally fake competencies but to realistically demonstrate them when critical. Doing so cements others' trust in your comprehensive capabilities as much as raw persona.

With both less-polished elements refinished and innate strengths spotlighted, you craft executive communication able to spur belief across diverse onlookers. Leadership grows through effortful self-improvement as much as playing to nature's gifts.

Accounting for Perception Biases

Unfortunately, leadership communication sometimes miscarries due to audience preconceptions outside any leader's control. Gender, ethnic and other biases unconsciously color how groups perceive identical words or deeds.

A leader excelling in qualities like warmth may pass as competent by one demographic while considered inadequate by another. Same for straightforward speech reading as blunt depending on listener interpretative leanings.

When positional power cannot neutralize bias, proactively recruit team members exuding attributes you currently lack. Have them tackle scenarios demanding that strength, modeling well-rounded leadership. Additionally, bring biases to light neutrally in appropriate settings to lessen projection.

There is no eliminating biases but acknowledging gaps between intent and interpretations can render them less influential. Your leadership voice sounds fully when teams hear it unfiltered by preordained beliefs.

Finding Confidence to Lead as You Are

Insecurities often self-sabotage authentic leaders but take heart, battling nerves is universal. Yet frequently the root of stage fright lies in perceived divergence from our imaginary standards. We judge outselves harshly and thus mute our truest voices while grasping outward for external validation.

Remember, your leadership identity runs deeper than superficial traits. If you inspire anyone – subordinates, peers, friends – through being more you, build on that fact. Small acts of courage in leading as is stacks over time, replacing self-doubt with earned confidence.

Validation emerges from doing work meaningful to you boldly and through a lens only you possess. As traction grows, any imposter syndrome you may have will recede. Soon, you can lead through the same honesty that has been winning supporters all along privately.

Let go of seeking confirmation from abstract leader checklists. Instead know self-belief sediments into concrete capabilities through repeatedly exercising authentic voice. Your distinct leadership style awaits below fears of acting differently. Cast them off.

The path to commanding leadership communication resides inside each one of us. So, peel away layers of assumptions and uncertainty to reveal the motivating voice already there. Through acting on your abilities and improving gaps sincerely, you grow into your true executive presence.

Developing Leaders Through Mentorship

Leadership manifests in those able to bring out the highest potential in others. By mentoring team members through ongoing guidance, directors can exponentially expand enterprise capabilities while grooming the next generation. Whether through formal programs or informal interactions, mentorship fuels professional growth on both sides of the relationship.

Here, we will explore mentorship as a strategic leadership development mechanism. We will examine reverse mentoring benefits, transformational leadership characteristics modeled through mentoring, and specific steps leaders can take to foster productive mentor-mentee partnerships. While mentorship cultivates short-term performance gains, its true power emerges in strengthening organizational leadership pipelines over sustained periods.

Mentorship as a Two-Way Learning Conduit

A common misconception holds that mentors impart wisdom through one-way instruction. However, effective mentorship relies on reciprocal exchange between parties at different career stages. Through curiosity, perspectives widen for veterans and emerging talent alike, sparking refreshment and progress.

Take reverse mentoring for example, where senior executives partner with younger staff. By exploring new technologies, media, or cultural shifts, directors touch base with frontline experiences beyond the C-suite bubble. This outside-in view spurs more relevance to consumer meta-trends. Or, consider lateral mentoring between peers across functions. Here, insight sharing prevents siloed thinking, benefiting mentees as much as mentors.

At its core, impactful mentorship centers around Q&A, not lectures. When mentors adopt learning mindsets despite seniority, it manifests the intellectual stimulation and humility that characterizes resonant leadership. By modeling vulnerability in grappling with unfamiliar ideas, mentors humanize the journey ahead for mentees. In turn, rising professionals recognize their own growth potential through self-efficacy gains.

Mentorship Pathways to Transformational Leadership

Transformational directors motivate teams by connecting organizational objectives to employee aspirations. They boost confidence through encouragement while driving accountability for progress. Masterful mentors embody these same qualities. By focusing interactions on mentee needs and growth areas, they provide psychological safety to explore development. At the same time, they maintain high standards, structuring sessions around constructive feedback that stretches comfort zones.

This mentorship balance between compassion and challenge manifests the inspiration and influence central to transformational leadership. As mentees apply lessons from exchanges, their expanded capabilities ripple through teams to

multiply productivity gains. Furthermore, the care shown through individu-
alized attention builds loyalty and engagement.

Over time, the appreciation for mentorship received inspines mentees to pay
it forward. This propagation sustains organizational advancement as seasoned
professionals impart knowledge to emerging talent in a virtuous cycle. Soon,
mentorship flows through institutional veins, securing leadership continuity.

Steps to Foster Effective Mentorships

While chemistry cannot be forced, leaders can nurture mentorship by:

- Seeking broad mentee diversity

- Outlining development goals and guardrails upfront

- Driving frequent, constructive conversations

- Showing authentic interest in mentee perspectives

- Providing growth-oriented feedback

- Celebrating mentee progress and wins

Ultimately, leadership manifests in unlocking potential. Committing to mentorship multiplies talent development through an exchange both parties gain
from. By pouring knowledge and care into mentees, transformational leaders
empower the entire organization's future.

Mentorship's downstream benefits surface in those you help propel just as
much as your own continued growth through reverse exchange. As mentees
blossom into influential directors themselves, organizations profit from compounding returns on mentor leadership. Of course, leaders must balance nu-
merous priorities, but regular one-on-one sessions with emerging professionals
represent worthy investments given mentorship's multiplying power. Soon,

your greatest payout will arise as rising talent carries the torch even further through the flames first kindled within them.

The Critical Role of Mentors in Leadership Journeys

Mentorship forms the backbone of impactful leadership development, providing rising professionals with trusted guidance to realize their potential. Forward-thinking organizations must strategically foster mentor-mentee partnerships as a talent progression pipeline investment that yields exponential returns.

Mentors accelerate competency development, provide psychological safety nets, create networking conduits, and nurture accountabilities that yield leadership excellence. While mentoring requires resource commitments, developing next-generation leaders who live and breathe company values sustains long-term prosperity.

Navigating Leadership Complexity

Transitioning into leadership roles brings wholly unfamiliar terrain with ever-shifting conditions to adapt to. The predictable career trajectories mentees enjoyed as individual contributors no longer apply, which can overwhelm despite innate talents. Imposter syndrome runs rampant with first-time leadership, especially for historically marginalized groups overcoming systemic barriers.

This is where mentors provide critical guidance grounded in lived experience. They help mentees process complex emotions, normalize doubt, and build resilience by sharing their own winding leadership journeys. Through advice, encouragement, and empathy, mentors provide mental safety nets for risk-taking essential for growth. By inspiring self-belief, they turn self-limiting assumptions into launching pads for realizing potential.

Importantly, mentors go beyond emotional support to spur tangible competency development. As strategic soundboards, they prompt critical reflection to shape well-rounded thinking and instincts. Mentees surface blindspots while analyzing scenarios from multiple vantage points, preparing them to lead amid ambiguity. Furthermore, mentors transfer contextual knowledge around company politics, unwritten rules, and relationship building that enables smooth transitions into director-level roles.

Opening Doors through Networks

Mentors also provide visibility and connections within organizations due to their extensive professional networks cultivated over years. By introducing mentees to decision-makers across business units and functions, they facilitate exponential relationship-building opportunities. Even small gestures like forwarding mentee resumes or regularly referencing their work builds profile visibility that opens career doors.

Of course, mentors determine high-potential talent mainly through consistent excellence rather than mere exposure. As such, they maintain accountability by setting stretching goals then tracking progress through regular check-ins. This prevents mentees from resting on their laurels while keeping development front and center. Constructive feedback around growth areas coupled with acknowledging wins sustains forward momentum. Soon, mentees echo these same standards with their own teams, perpetuating cycles of high performance.

In this sense, committed mentoring underpins a thriving leadership culture focused on unlocking potential. Passing wisdom to emerging talent sustains organizations by ensuring continuity even as individual directors come and go. In fact, the number of leadership mentors often serves as the best predictor of enterprise advancement.

Leadership carries ultimate accountability for moving organizations forward. However, directors cannot shoulder this responsibility alone. It takes a village to develop well-rounded, ethical leaders worth entrusting the future to. Embedding mentoring as an cultural pillar allows each generation to build on the last. Of course, mentoring requires investments like designated time, program oversight, and mentor training. But molding even a handful of principled proteges already yields exponential returns through sustained excellence.

Key Takeaways & Final Thoughts on Cultivating Impactful Leadership

Key Takeaways:

- Leadership development is an ongoing journey that requires balancing technical expertise and people skills. Understand expectations at each career level and proactively build skills for next level roles.

- Leadership capabilities manifest at every organizational tier, not just the C-suite. Demonstrating diligence and reliability early on lays foundations for greater responsibilities.

- As leaders become more senior, expectations shift from task reliability toward strategic orientation, team inspiration, and change management capabilities.

- Realizing leadership as a continuous, adaptive process allows professionals to actively shape satisfying careers. Identify current gaps and refine abilities before next-level demands arise.

- There are many leadership styles - visionary, coaching, servant, autocratic etc. Savvy leaders blend styles fluidly depending on contexts, stakeholders and challenges.

- A leader's communication style sets the tone for team behaviors. Clearly convey expectations through words and actions to empower peak performance.

- Optimal leadership communication requires sending unified messages about values and vision through aligned styles and explicit requests.

- Insecurities often sabotage authentic leaders. Build confidence through small acts of courage in communicating genuinely over time. Your unique leadership style awaits.

- Mentoring delivers reciprocating benefits for both mentors and mentees. Mentees gain role modeling, advice, access to networks, and accountability structures that fast-track competency building. Meanwhile, mentors receive reverse mentoring through fresh perspectives that combat insular thinking.

- Transformational leadership aims to motivate teams by connecting organizational objectives to employee aspirations. Masterful mentors manifest these same qualities by focusing on unlocking potential through support and challenge. Their influence cascades through mentees who pay it forward.

- Impactful leadership mentoring centers on crafting two-way developmental relationships rather than one-way knowledge flow. It relies on high engagement, clearly defined expectations, tangible support, and sustained commitment from both parties.

- Mentorship serves as a powerful talent progression pipeline that sustains enterprises over time. Passing wisdom across generations embeds leadership capabilities and perpetuates cultures of excellence.

The Winding Path of Leadership Development

Few leadership journeys follow straightforward progressions. Promising individual contributors often flounder after moving into people manager roles only to reclaim high-flyer trajectories years later after self-reflection. Seasoned executives, in turn, risk falling into conventions that fail to resonate with evolving market realities. Ripening into an impactful leader calls for continual renewal rather than formulaic arrival.

As such, formal and experiential learning both play critical roles given their complementary strengths. Academics provide structured approaches to digest leadership theories and case studies. However, abstract concepts alone fail to deliver nuanced appreciation of directing complex teams towards shared visions. On the other hand, real-world exposure builds instincts through trial-and-error yet often lacks frameworks to accurately assess experiences.

This is where high-impact mentorship bridges understanding gaps for leadership aspirants through contextualized guidance. Mentors take conceptual models and ground them in specifics situations, allowing mentees to deeply internalize how aligned leadership philosophies manifest in practice. They provide psychological safety nets for early-career professionals navigating unfamiliar organizational dynamics while prompting critical reflection that broadens perspectives.

Transitioning into leadership roles brings wholly unfamiliar terrain to navigate. Self-doubt runs rampant even for high-potentials without adequate guidance. This is where mentors provide situational insights and emotional scaffolding grounded in lived experience. By illuminating organizational dynamics through storytelling, they bolster mentee resilience while fast-tracking contextual competency development beyond theoretical knowledge. Soon mentees pay forward support received to peers and direct reports, propagating empowered cultures organization-wide.

Impactful leaders never cease their own development journeys. They lean on guidance from peer mentors across fields and industries to widen aperture and benchmark strategies. And they dedicate themselves to illuminating pathways for emerging talents, driven by the multiplicative advances that ripple through enterprises when even a single mentee blossoms.

The continual renewal mentorship sparks at personal and organizational levels highlights leadership as a lifelong practice rather than a status summit. We must acknowledge the mentors who shone light along our way and pay it forward so aspiring mentees may carry the torch even further tomorrow. The cycle continues but the compounding returns only grow. Where will your leadership journey lead?

Chapter Two

Navigating the Dynamics of Success

S uccess in any organization is a complex equation. As leaders, our career trajectories largely depend upon our ability not just to deliver results, but to do so in line with particular workplace "rules of the game." Much as we might wish otherwise, these rules are often unspoken and shaped by forces beyond our direct control.

And yet understanding them matters immensely. Those individuals who consistently "win" at organizational politics and gain advancement tend to have mastered both formal evaluation criteria and informal norms around risk-taking, creativity, relationship-building and more. However, while studying these trends can provide a roadmap for rising through the ranks, that path may not always align with our values or prove personally sustainable.

So what is a well-intentioned leader to do? How do we reconcile understanding —and even employing—an organization's rules of success with staying true to ourselves?

The answer lies in cultivating the two cornerstones of sustainable success: *self-awareness* and *adaptability*. By regularly reflecting upon our priorities and abilities within shifting contexts, we give ourselves the chance to make deliberate choices. We maintain agency rather than simply allowing factors outside ourselves—a boss's opinion, a company's cultural biases—to dictate our path.

The following strategies can support leaders seeking sustainable advancement without sacrificing integrity:

Assess the Rules of Success

Organizational dynamics rarely align seamlessly with formal processes and evaluation metrics. Take time to discern not just official pathways for advancement but also the unspoken norms, relationships, skill-sets and behaviors that enable certain individuals to consistently gain influence and rewards.

While official criteria offer one clue (for example, linking bonuses to cost-savings or new sales), also look at who specifically earns promotions and plum assignments. Talk to trusted colleagues about trends they perceive. Identify those skill-sets most handsomely compensated. What "horse trading" occurs behind the scenes?

As an additional prompt, reflect upon key areas where your organization appears to prioritize contradictory goals. Do nay-sayers get ahead faster than innovators? Are critics or "yes" men more likely to succeed? Understanding where and why inconsistencies arise will illuminate unseen values driving decisions.

Check Alignment with Personal Values

Once you have mapped out the often unspoken requirements for advancement in your workplace, thoughtfully consider alignment with your personal values and priorities. This clarity is essential because the stresses of conforming to competing demands day after day, year after year, take a toll. Resentment builds. Health suffers. Talented leaders exit.

Rather than simply reacting, spend time in self-reflection. Are there elements of your organization's success metrics resonating for you? You may discover shared values that make conformity less draining. Or you might determine certain behaviors so egregious you cannot sustain them without feeling inauthentic. There are no right answers, merely those that feel truthful for your evolving self.

Embrace Adaptability

Perhaps nothing accelerates career advancement more powerfully than strategically employing adaptability. The paradox lies in discerning when to conform to organizational rules of success and when standing firm in your own vision serves you better.

Navigating these decisions requires growing comfortable with complexity. Absolute truths provide less traction than responsive attention to evolving contexts and skill sets. Set priorities not by blindly following static rules but based on regular check-ins with your ambitions and values. Adapt behaviors without compromising personal ethics. Seek work aligned with strengths and interests, even when it contradicts standard paths.

The organizations most hungry for leaders exhibit similar traits of self-examination and flexibility themselves. Bureaucratic environments that incentivize checking boxes over creative solutions offer fewer opportunities for advancement. But learning to reframe challenges, collaborate across differences and mentor struggling co-workers builds positive momentum regardless. Savvy leaders recognize that sustainable success relies on continually upskilling, forming trust-based networks and focusing attention on the positives.

Attempting an organizational short-cut by perfectly calibrating to its spoken and unspoken "rules of success" rarely pays off long-term. Resilient leaders instead prioritize self-awareness, adapt driectly with integrity and lead through service. While initially this approach requires more effort, it builds skills and relationships transferrable across contexts. You expand influence based on social capital rather than politics. And you avoid the cynicism and resentment plaguing those who compromise values while scrambling upwards.

Of course, the path of integrity holds no guarantees. But leaders who focus on sustainable self-growth tend to attract opportunities anyway, often emerging as their organization's guiding lights when the terrain inevitably shifts. So take time to honestly assess your workplace's values, reflect upon alignment with your own and embrace adaptability as a muscle to continually strengthen. Chart your course based on passion plus principle rather than simply conforming to broken systems. With resilience and patience, you will find the organizational dynamics well suited for your gifts or have the experience to manifest an environment that is. Either way, you step forward with personal integrity intact.

Defining Your Leadership Path

Navigating any career involves making choices. Some decisions respond to external structures—educational requirements, pay scales, cultural norms. Others allow us to manifest inner visions—our talents, values and priorities.

Professional goal-setting draws upon both frames of reference. Unlike personal objectives centered on lifestyle, relationships or wellness, career aspirations directly correlate to workplace achievement. They motivate us in tangible ways. The path seems clearer.

And yet, within these practical bounds, possibility exists to create space for self-expression. Beyond formal incentives pushing us forward, we can identify meaningful professional objectives resonating internally as well.

The goals we commit to profoundly impact daily experiences. More consciously balancing external and internal motivations allows for staying power. Environments that throttle creativity and meaning inevitably take their toll, wearing us down. But settings welcoming our whole selves unlock potential, opening doors wider than we may have imagined.

Defining Your Path

Begin by taking stock of professional credentials required for advancement in fields of interest. These structural elements—additional degrees, certifications, technical competencies—comprise the skeleton of goal-setting.

Yet don't stop here. Look for windows to tailor objectives around innate strengths and joys as well. Opportunities abound to develop skills, projects and leadership roles resonating deeply as expressions of your best self.

Finally, recognize professional goals as flexible guides rather than rigid constraints. Revisiting dreams periodically allows for natural evolution in perspective. What energized us at twenty may differ from forty. And maintaining space for spontaneity means saying yes when unexpected doors open.

The Intent Behind the Path

More empowering than the exact finish line is discovering the purpose fueling your journey there. Professional objectives rooted in your unique abilities and values direct your days with meaning. They drive you to grow through challenge rather than turn rigid chasing rewards alone.

So take time for self-reflection as you clarify next steps. What underlying motivations shape your aspirations? How might you redefine career milestones as celebrations of internal strengths rather than just external achievement?

Your intentions transform the path itself. When professional goals give voice to your highest self, you walk with growing confidence and clarity. Not despite uncertainty but because of it.

Charting Your Leadership Course

Reaching for our highest vision always requires taking concrete steps. Even expansive dreams manifest through focused intentionality. Luck plays some part, certainly, but achievement mostly relies on skillfully navigating day-to-day choices in service of our larger aims.

With so many competing priorities, establishing structure empowers progress and change. We transform nebulous hopes into defined goals. And then construct checklists guiding us forward with clarity and consistency.

Of course, executing any plan requires periodic reassessment as well. By consciously analyzing what propels or blocks us, we can release outdated assumptions and reorient towards possibility once more. Our goals act as compasses rather than chains—flexible guides grounded in authentic truth rather than rigid metrics determining worth.

This responsive approach allows for continually clarifying unique expressions of excellence. Understanding when to stay the course and when to change trajectory relies less on formula and more on self-awareness cultivated through consistent reflection.

What steps empower your highest potential not just for worldly markers of "success" but for fulfillment grounded in purposeful living? Let these key strategies guide and affirm your personal path ahead.

Finding Your North Star

Beyond surface aims, leaders uncover underlying motivations by contemplating deeper questions. Finding one's North Star relies on introspection aptly illuminating life priorities and core values.

Commit to truthful self-inquiry through tools like journaling. Consider what energizes and fulfills you beyond titles or salary alone. Do certain subject matters, problem types or interpersonal dynamics engage your interests and strengths consistently? Reflecting on patterns of intrinsic reward reveals talent affinities and source codes for meaning. Documenting discoveries forms a foundation clarifying professional paths intrinsically worthwhile.

Unearthing Core Values: Core values signify principles guiding conduct and choices. To identify yours, envision life circumstances challenging your integrity. Which non-negotiables consistently surface during tumult? Contemplate exemplars admiring their virtuous qualities. Note traits driving their decisions illuminating your own moral compass. Discussing values with trusted confidants provides outsider perspective aiding self-awareness. Once discerned, regularly revisit your top priorities ensuring consistency.

Envisioning an Authentic Existence: With motivations and virtues surfaced, contemplate life experiences fueling fulfillment. What contributions uplift others and affirm your humanity? Imagine achieving hopes creatively impacting positive change. Crafting vision statements or future memoirs expressing soulful aims inspires purposeful living. Regularly reflect on manifestations bringing daily actions into alignment with your North Star.

Actualizing Guidance: This grounding self-knowledge informs meaningful goal-setting. Track progress qualitatively through journals emphasizing lessons and connections rather than tasks alone. Upend routines replenishing inspiration. Surround yourself with allies supporting growth into one's highest self. Maintaining awareness of purpose amid obstacles keeps minor setbacks in perspective, fortifying determination to live fully through work. Finding one's North Star creates an enduring compass for navigation.

Mapping the Path

With larger purpose clarified, thoughtfully identify short and longer-term goals manifesting this aim. Divide intimidating milestones into incremental objectives with clear metrics for success. These measurable guideposts mark progress, fueling motivation during inevitable slogs.

Remember to balance different spheres of living within your plan—career, relationships, self-care, community, and other realms interweave rather than compete when grounded in common purpose. Schedule regular check-ins to celebrate wins, course correct where needed, and update targets relative to life's changing shape.

Staying the Course

Consistency proves challenging even with the clearest roadmap. Distractions arise, priorities shift and progress stalls. Self-discipline wavers. Rather than judging natural ups and downs, recognize oscillations as a waypoint for pausing and recentering.

Use periods of stagnation or frustration as a signal to stop striving and intentionally reconnect. What initially sparked this goal? Is the underlying aim still resonant? Reaffirm your commitment or release outdated expectations with self-compassion. Then refresh the actions propelling you onward or revise plans aligned with evolved understanding.

By continually clarifying purpose behind concrete goals, we build energy banks sustaining us through temporary obstacles. Each step leads us back to our North Star, illuminating the path ahead with renewed inspiration.

Leading Through Limits

Leading well relies on continually clarifying vision. Not just formulating strategy but also understanding personal limits needing acknowledgment to manifest that strategy responsively. Knowing when to stretch beyond comfort and when to circle back for self-care empowers our most sustainable service.

In leadership especially, blurred boundaries exhaust precious mental, emotional and physical reserves. Without structure around availability, we leave little energy for proactive planning, creative innovation and the relational attunement undergirding organizational health.

Reestablishing boundaries relies first on self-awareness—recognizing over-extension—then self-advocacy in realigning relationships and schedules around authentic capacity. By clearly communicating limitations while continuing to hold space for connection, we model healthy transparency, upholding team empowerment along with our own.

The Benefits of Limits

Consider the value of structure in other creative endeavors. Artists speak of limitations forcing ingenuity. Poets describe form as liberating. Athletes leverage restraint to exceed perceived potential. What well-placed boundaries might empower your leadership and team to thrive?

Mental Focus: Frequent distractions and ad hoc demands prevent the mental spaciousness strategic thinking requires. Defining windows for deep work around planning, analysis and complex tasks allows cognitive capacity to recharge.

Emotional Energy: Pouring continuously into others' needs while neglecting your own inevitably breeds resentment and numbness. Blocking periods for rejuvenating reflection prevents compassion fatigue, keeping leadership resilient.

Sustainable Modeling: Demonstrating responsiveness 24/7 sets unrealistic expectations on behavior for emerging leaders. Establishing offline periods signals that integration of self-care with delivering results is non-negotiable.

Team Empowerment:
Excessive hand-holding breeds dependence rather than ownership. Structures promoting autonomous decision-making strengthen individuals' confidence and collective capability long-term.

Crafting Healthy Boundaries

Once recognizing overextension's diminishing returns, proactively communicating needed changes significantly eases realignment. Clearly convey the "why" before the "what" in establishing new norms.

State the Situation: Describe behaviors signaling you have overextended bandwidth - shortness, forgetfulness, depleted energy. Use "I" statements owning experience rather than blaming others.

Articulate Impacts: Connect situations directly to consequences - compromised strategic thinking, emotional fatigue, poor modeling for team members. These effects negatively reverberate across organization.

Define New Parameters: Based on impacts, state limitations needing acknowledgement moving forward while reaffirming care for team's growth. Perhaps this means defining "office hours" or instituting new protocols for accessing your time.

Implement Collaboratively: Invite team's input adjusting new boundaries to ease transition. Leverage natural pauses - start of month, post-milestone, etc. - to initiate changes flowing naturally from established workflow.

Address Resistance Compassionately: Some may struggle with new structures if they displace previous norms or power dynamics. Revisit "why's" of decisions and focus on mutual commitment to team's long-term thriving over short-term comfort.

Realigning through Limits

Establishing healthy boundaries relies first on recognizing the need for realignment through self-reflection, then compassionately communicating limits with those impacted. Maintaining transparency around "why" certain changes empower individual and collective potential smooths transitions.

Of course perfection matters less than progress. Setbacks will occur and require responsiveness in remapping boundaries aligned with evolving needs. Leading through limits is a continual practice grounded in wisdom deeper than rigid rules. By investing in this self-knowledge and skillful navigation, your best self and team can thrive in service of potential far greater than imagined.

Leading in the Flow

The pace of modern work culture exacts a toll. Endless demands and distractions exert pressure to continually do more faster, keeping leaders in a state of chronic reactivity. Overwork gets conflated with effectiveness despite diminishing returns. We forget why all the striving matters in the first place.

Yet sustainably navigating workflow relies less on rallying more effort than on realigning attention with what truly matters. By working consciously rather than reflexively, we transform frenzied activity into energized flow states aligned with authentic priorities.

The Difference Between Busyness and Flow
Chronic overwhelm signals misalignment between activities, energy and values. Despite diligently employing time management best practices, leaders remain stuck in unsustainable patterns.

The problem lies less in specific strategies than the frenetic mindset behind them. Approaching time as a scarce commodity to hoard fuels self-judgment and depletion rather than creative engagement. Leaders stay busy yet distracted from purpose.

In contrast, flow activity channels focus without congestion. By fully committing presence to one meaningful task, we gain traction even in limited increments. The key rests in continually clarifying underlying motivations toward which we consciously direct attention hour to hour, day to day.

1. Flow Follows The Energy

Rather than forcing unnatural momentum, leverage natural energy cycles for optimal efficiency. Map typical mental/emotional rhythms across days and weeks, aligning focused efforts with peak flow states when concentration clicks. Schedule mundane tasks requiring less mental acuity during downs.

2. Flow Serves The Purpose

Continually connect daily objectives to overarching organizational vision for motivation and meaning. Whether drafting a status report or resolving conflict, recall intended impact toward shared goals, allowing leadership to feel purposeful despite inevitable drudgery.

3. Flow Requires Presence

With so many distractions, directors and managers easily lose hours down digital rabbit holes. Curtail aimless browsing to inhabit TRUE priorities with aliveness. When present, even mundane steps gain traction. When distracted, even glamorous efforts stall.

4. Flow Respects Humanity

The myth of robotic, 24/7 productivity discounts basic human needs which inevitably assert themselves unmet. Rather than reactively playing catchup once exhausted, proactively integrate downshifts. Whether 5-minute dance breaks or screening afternoons for renewal, self-care prevents system-wide burnout.

Sustainably navigating task overload relies less on Herculean effort than incremental realignment toward energized service of what matters most. When pressed by demands, reconnect with core motivations fueling higher purpose. When overextended, retreat just long enough for refreshed reengagement. By modeling such conscientious leadership, teams transform frenetic patterns into satisfying flow. Together, redirect from distraction toward traction. From depletion toward inspired action. From joyless rat races to purposeful progress through empowered presence.

The burdens of responsibility need not overwhelm. By leading through flow, we walk our talk of workplace cultures where engaged contribution breeds fulfillment rather than fatigue.

Key Takeaways & Final Thoughts on Navigating the Dynamics of Success

Key Takeaways:

- Success relies on continually clarifying alignment between personal values and organizational norms

- Regular self-reflection allows responding to competing priorities with wisdom rather than reaction

- Embracing complexity empowers sustainable navigation of workplace dynamics

- Clearly communicating needed boundaries transforms cultures toward collective thriving

- Redirecting from distraction toward conscious flow liberates energy for what matters most

Far from a straight path, leadership calls us into growth as we walk routes revealing themselves step by step. Demands and duties exhaust when addressed as burdens detached from meaning. But grounded in purpose, they energize, directing efforts toward service much larger than ourselves.

Of course we all fall short despite best aims. Responsibilities conflict with care for self and others. Integrity wavers amidst pressures real and perceived.

And still, more empowering than any single right choice is cultivating presence attuned to what matters most in each new moment. By continually reconnecting with wisdom deeper than personal preference, we gain strength for moving forward together beyond surface tension into possibility.

The way rarely appears clearly lit. Yet when leaders shine light inward for guidance and ground decisions in core values, integrity finds embodiment through us, lighting the path ahead.

However imperfectly, we walk our talk.

Chapter Three

Building Your Leadership Career

Your career trajectory deeply impacts your life's journey. Yet many leaders feel stuck on autopilot, passively going through the motions without a clear flight plan. Constructing an intentional career strategy is instrumental for reaching your highest leadership potential while maintaining resilience in the face of inevitable obstacles. This requires understanding your career as a lifelong marathon punctuated by periods of rapid growth, stability, and even strategic retreat. With the right mindset and strategies, you can take the pilot's seat to build a leadership career that aligns with your values and aspirations.

Assessing Organizational Fit

Choosing where to devote your leadership capacity may be one of the most monumental decisions in shaping your career journey. Seek employers poised for growth and alignment with your long-term goals. Forward-looking organizations allow space for leaders to develop new capabilities while expanding their impact. Evaluate an employer's stability, competitiveness, workplace culture, training opportunities, and whether the experience will be valuable for your future roles. Avoid boxed-in niche expertise with limited transferable application. Instead, gain exposure to universal leadership skills like strategic thinking, cross-functional collaboration, change management, and coaching team members.

Organizations hire leaders to move teams forward. But titles alone will not ensure impact or advancement. Take an honest assessment of whether you can successfully fill a role based on the employer's expectations and indicators for success. Have candid conversations with leadership about how they envision your contributions. Shoring up executive sponsorships also provides visibility for potential promotions. Remember that many leaders plateau when organizational needs evolve beyond their capabilities. Continually expanding your leadership toolkit prepares you to progress in step with company growth.

Developing High-Visibility Projects

All leaders seek opportunities to guide critical initiatives with broad influence. But simply waiting to be handed a high-profile project is not a reliable strategy. Elevate your visibility by spearheading work that addresses organizational pain points and gaps. What emerging priorities align with your expertise and interests? Brainstorm project ideas using trend reports, customer feedback, and financial results, then make a case for resources.

Once you secure leadership support, apply robust project management discipline to inspire stakeholder confidence. Leverage change management models to bring colleagues along each phase, quantifying success through OKRs. Although steering prominent projects involves risk, leaders must break through the fear of failure that stifles bold innovation. Reframe setbacks as progress by quickly course correcting based on feedback. Completing complex deliverables demonstrates your expanding capabilities, showcasing your leadership to key decision makers. But beware of solely focusing inwards. Make time to engage externally through speaking events, media interviews and building strategic partnerships.

Choosing Values-Aligned Leadership Roles

As you advance into senior management, increased visibility comes under intense public scrutiny. Authentic, values-driven leaders attract support by taking a ethical and compassionate stance. Before accepting an executive role, extensively evaluate the company's track record and transparency around ethical issues like sustainability, governance scandals, harmful products or labor relations. Representing an organization perceived as unethical can torpedo your credibility as a leader.

Similarly, reflect on whether an employer's values and priorities align with your leadership purpose. Leadership requires conviction; advocating for goals you don't believe in breeds cynicism and burnout. Construct your career journey around leading causes that energize you. If current leadership seems misaligned, maintain resilience by strengthening peer connections, mentoring emerging talent and highlighting counter perspectives. With an empowering leadership network and results that speak for themselves, you expand options for making a positive difference through new roles.

By taking decisive action at critical junctures, you can build your leadership career with intention instead of indifference. Define the destination by clarifying your values, capabilities and impact goals. Set your trajectory in motion by selecting growth-oriented employers that empower leaders. And finally, actively strengthen your personal brand by delivering visible projects that make progress on organizational priorities. With the resilience to learn from obstacles along the way, you can take charge of your leadership journey.

Capitalizing on Your Leadership Strengths

As a leader guiding your team through almost constant change, leverage your unique strengths to maximize impact. Rather than dwelling on weaknesses, build innovation upon existing capabilities.

Take Inventory of Strengths

Intimately knowing your strengths provides clarity when navigating uncharted waters. Reflect on when you have felt fully energized, completely in flow, and filled with conviction. What activities, environments, and roles unlocked this level of engagement? Was it rallying people around a vision, creating new frameworks, or spearheading a turnaround? Pinpoint the leadership muscles you instinctively flex and then stretch.

Catalog feedback from your mentors, peers, and direct reports highlighting your leadership superpowers. Synthesize this input to reveal overarching themes that form your leadership DNA. Do you excel at cultivating talent, executing strategies, or transforming teams? Perhaps you possess rare expertise or excel at building partnerships. By clearly naming your strengths, you codify your leadership brand.

Maximize Time in the Strength Zone

With clarity on your areas of excellence, reorient your calendar to spend more hours playing to your leadership strengths. Delegate or outsource complementary capabilities that drain precious time and energy. Refocus meeting agendas on leading strategy discussions or coaching colleagues instead of simply reporting status.

Set ambitious goals that specifically leverage your strengths to create breakthroughs. What change could you catalyze across the organization if you doubled down on your superpower? Allow your strengths to shape decision making by assessing new projects and tasks through this lens. If something fails to utilize your sweet spot, is it wise to accept or could someone else better shoulder that role? Your strength zone is the launch pad for the unique impact only you can make.

Broaden Capacity Around Strengths

While avoiding overextension, push beyond your comfort zone to broaden the application of your strengths. How could you flex these muscles in innovative ways to spur transformation? Could you inspire movement on stalled priorities by rallying and aligning leaders? Or breakthrough siloed mindsets by facilitating cross-functional collaboration? Instead of leaving your strengths isolated in a single initiative, discover how to weave this capability throughout the organizational fabric.

Leading through continuous change requires playing to your strengths while minimizing time fighting against your weaker capabilities. Define and then capitalize on your leadership superpowers to maximize your performance, engagement and fulfillment.

Strategically Planning Your Leadership Career

Navigating a fulfilling career requires intention and skill much like captaining a ship across the ocean. Without a well-defined destination or navigation plan, you risk drifting off course. Define your professional north star by clarifying strengths, values and motivators. Equip yourself for the journey ahead by shoring up skills and connections. Maintain resilience in the face of obstacles by course-correcting towards opportunities aligned with your purpose.

Approach each role as a voyage that builds capacities for where you want to go. Establish short term goals to build specific skills and relationships that serve long term aims. Seize assignments that increase leadership scope and visibility among decision makers. Have the courage to course correct when better alignments with your purpose appear.

This is best demonstrated as an 8-step process for crafting a personalized career plan, with each step examined in-depth. By understanding one's strengths, interests, opportunities and goals, individuals can chart a purposeful path for professional growth and success.

Step 1: Review Your Strengths, Weaknesses, Motivators, and Values

The first and most vital step is honest self-reflection. Thorough self-analysis allows one to build upon strengths while addressing weakness. Tools like the Personal SWOT Analysis aid this process. Beyond skills, understanding motivators through frameworks like Schein's Career Anchors reveals what work energizes and fulfills us. Clarifying core values through models such as the top five values exercise provides an ethical compass. This groundwork yields crucial self-insights that inform all subsequent career decisions.

Step 2: Know Your Comparative Advantage

With self-awareness cultivated, the next key is determining one's unique value proposition. While innate abilities and developed expertise surely exist, comparative advantage concerns that which distinguishes you specifically within a given environment. Recall strengths regularly reinforced in reviews. Solicit colleague perspectives respectfully. Your comparative edge fills a niche demand and fuels competitive differentiation if optimized.

Step 3: Research Possibilities and Make the Most of Opportunities

A Personal PEST (Political, Economic, Social, and Tech) Analysis scans macro influences that environmental scanning considers political, economic, social, and technological changes impacting an industry. Similarly, revisiting one's SWOT highlights strength-driven opportunities internally. Proactively developing through employer-funded education demonstrates initiative while expanding skillsets. Experienced mentors offer invaluable guidance if an advising relationship is mutually beneficial.

Step 4: Develop Expertise

By envisioning aspirations informed by self-knowledge, the training and qualifications necessary will emerge. Accreditations, continuing education courses, leadership programs - various pathways exist to sharpen applicable expertise over time. Commitment to lifelong learning ensures careers evolve along with the ever-changing nature of work. Mastery comes from focused efforts to augment strengths identified in prior reflection.

Step 5: Network

As the adage notes, "It's not what you know, it's who you know." Wise networking expands one's professional community and visibility. Within and beyond the organization, cultivate relationships industry-wide by lending support as often as receiving it. Electronic networks like LinkedIn have become valuable strategic alliance-building tools. Give generously of informational resources and referrals for networking's full benefits.

Step 6: Analyze Current Options

Always searching for growth opportunities, consider internal projects allowing display of unique abilities. Volunteer leadership roles provide testing grounds. Craft duties emphasizing targeted skills. Creatively configuring one's position through discussion with leaders can optimize development. Short-term adjustments may position long-term success. Maintain a mindset open to serendipitous chances.

Step 7: Pull It All Together

Periodic reviews integrate discoveries at each step. Reflection ensures self-awareness remains accurate. Cross-examining motivations, strengths, network, and options indicates a direction aligned with talents and values. Documenting conclusions creates a point of reference for evaluating altered circumstances. Continuous re-evaluation furthers understanding of one's evolving work constitution.

Step 8: Move Forward

With insight and intention, set tangible professional objectives. Divide goals into immediate and long-range targets. Monitor progress regularly while modifying plans as needed responsively. View setbacks not as failure but feedback.

Maintain momentum toward a purposeful career vision crafted through diligent self-examination and strategic implementation. Transparent career management sustains engagement and rewards fulfillment.

Developing an authentic personal career strategy demands an investment in self-knowledge. The iterative 8-step approach presented here supplies a framework for ongoing career cultivation. Regular reassessment and adaptation to changes internal or external ensures relevance and forward progression. Ultimately, a personalized approach to career management yields professional pathways as distinctive and vibrant as the individuals who design them.

Mastering Your Field

Navigating an ever-changing professional landscape requires continually expanding your expertise to adapt to emerging trends. Leaders must intimately understand their industry's evolution to guide teams through volatility and capitalize on opportunities. By immersing yourself within your field, you strengthen strategic thinking, client relationships, and career mobility.

Sharpening Your Strategic Edge

Strategy flows from a nuanced synthesis of internal and external dynamics. As the pace of change accelerates across industries, professionals risk advising teams from an outdated vantage point. Without a pulse on technological innovations, customer expectations, competition moves or regulatory shifts, you operate in the dark. Leaders who actively monitor their landscape make accurate forecasts and quickly realign priorities.

Routinely carve out time to research industry reports, news and perspectives. Follow recognized thought leaders sharing cutting-edge research. Identify publications, podcasts and events that provide glimpses into the future. Monitor the strategies of pioneers pushing boundaries in adjacent spaces ripe for exchange. Distill signals from noise by reflecting on observations and asking, "What does this mean for us?"

Earning Client Trust

Savvy clients seek advisors immersed in the latest market innovations who can expertly guide strategy. By showcasing your dedication to mastering emerging technologies, tools and methodologies, you establish credibility. Clients need reassurance you can implement solutions that deliver ROI and enduring advantage.

Schedule meetings to share research on pilot programs, new product features and updated best practices that would benefit them. Then actively listen to challenges and co-develop test initiatives. Follow up with resources and connections that support collaboration. When clients view you as an invaluable navigator versus a vendor, you strengthen strategic partnerships.

Surfacing Creative Solutions

Immersing yourself within industry discourse sparks creative connections impossible in isolation. You begin noticing interconnected patterns, transferring solutions across contexts and blending diverse concepts. When actively problems solving, this cross-pollination unlocks innovation. Carry a notebook to capture flashes of inspiration from events or articles. Revisit notes later to connect ideas and explore potential projects. Browse industry journals outside your specialty to import fresh perspectives. Infusing broad inspiration with focused expertise breeds visionary leadership.

Career Mobility

While mastery of one niche provides job security, agility across specialties ensures mobility. Professionals who narrowly focus their development get stuck when functions evolve. But those who cultivate transferable skills quickly pivot into new roles.

Demonstrate versatility by leading cross-functional initiatives, breadth through conferences and depth via certificates. Identify missing capabilities for aspired positions and craft projects to evidence them. This showcases your expanding value beyond a single function. With visibility and validity across specializations, you receive preferential treatment for coveted opportunities.

In dynamic times, leaders must match the pace of change through dedicated learning. Immersing yourself within industry discourse enables strategic foresight, client trust, creative solutions and career optionality. By actively probing your professional frontier, you narrow the gap between current reality and future possibility.

Creating a Personal Brand

A distinguished personal brand accelerates influence and opens doors to game-changing opportunities. Clearly conveying your leadership identity attracts allies who resonate with your vision while differentiating you from peers. By aligning messaging and action around your authentic strengths and passions, you gain discretionary effort from teams inspired by your purpose.

Clarifying Your Essence

The foundation for an influential personal brand is an intimate understanding of your nature and aspirations. Reflect on the change you most want to make in the world. Why does this impact matter and compel you into leadership? Use this clarity of purpose as a North Star guiding your priorities and positions.

Catalog your leadership principles and non-negotiable values. What behaviors and beliefs can you never betray regardless of incentives or consequences? These convictions forge reputations of integrity that attract other ethical leaders.

Make an honest assessment of capabilities and impact you want to be known for. What evidence demonstrates this expertise such as client outcomes, publications and speaking engagements? The intersection of skills, values and purpose establishes your leadership DNA.

Conveying Your Brand

With clarity on your leadership essence, ensure alignment between identity and expression across communication channels. Craft an online presence that moves beyond qualifications to share principles and aspirations. Showcase leadership perspectives and culture philosophy through blogging and social media. Pursue speaking engagements that exemplify your brand aligned with target audiences and venues.

While leveraging digital platforms, don't neglect in-person relationship building. Attend conferences and events that convene your community. Introduce yourself to recognized figures and find common ground around values and ideas. Offer to support their initiatives through volunteering and amplifying their work. These organic connections meaningfully convey essence while developing partnerships.

Champion emerging leaders who embody your brand. Nominate them for awards, collaborate on projects, and advocate their advancement. Your brand lives through those you empower to carry your principles forward.

Reinforcing Over Time

Consistency and courage reinforce your leadership brand through volatility. Seek input from a leadership coach or trusted advisors on upholding integrity. Collect feedback from mentees on your adherence toValues and continually realign. Publicly address missteps with accountability to reinforce principles.

Continue expanding breadth and depth on the change you champion. Pursue continual learning and self reflection to evolve perspectives. Regularly update your messaging across platforms with new initiatives, ideas and calls to action.

The long arc of leadership requires flexible consistency grounded in self awareness. By clearly conveying and reinforcing your authentic principles and purpose over time, you galvanize others to expand your positive impact.

Key Takeaways & Final Thoughts on Building Your Leadership Career

Key Takeaways:

- Effective career navigation relies on clearly defining your inner compass based on strengths, passions and values to guide decision making. Maintaining an accurate understanding of your leadership brand attracts opportunities aligned with your purpose.

- Satisfaction and advancement require proactive preparation for possibilities before they fully form. Intentional development of missing capabilities and strategic networking expand available options.

- Change is a constant throughout industries and enterprises. Leaders who continually expand perspective and skills while demonstrating agility and integrity can pivot into emerging roles.

- Your legacy lives through talent you develop, knowledge you disseminate and culture you embed that outlasts your tenure. Leaving this lasting impact cements your voyage.

- Career trajectories rarely follow linear paths but rather cycle through seasons of stability, rapid growth and strategic retreat. Defining North Stars allows course correcting towards fulfillment.

An Ongoing Voyage of Leadership Discovery

Careers that utilize potential and align with purpose rarely unfold predictably. Professionals risk stagnation when passively adhering to prescribed paths versus deliberately charting their own courses. Some abandon early leadership in frustration only to discover untapped talents years later that propel their influence to new heights. Others achieve positions of authority but lose site of their essence and stall out. True fulfillment comes from within, not bestowed through external validations.

The continual change leaders must navigate in a volatile world demands lifelong learning agility. Static knowledge has an ever-shortening half-life before growing obsolete. Leaders who engage diverse perspectives through broad reading, events and mentors augment their instinct. They build resilience by challenging assumptions and enhancing awareness of interconnections.

Strategic leaders also take an entrepreneurial approach in managing their careers. They understand transitions into new challenges enable exponential growth at the expense of short-term comfort. They prepare through targeted skill building and relationship cultivation long before catalyzing such moves. And they architect roles that align with their strengths and motivations.

But lasting fulfillment stems not just from personalized success but also the legacy imprinted on human lives uplifted. It arises from embedding aspects of positive culture through knowledge transfer, talent progression and ecosystem influence - manifestations of purpose that persist. The voyages shaping our legacies rarely follow straight courses but leaders who define their essence and align values to direct development can captain careers through the inevitable ebbs and flows to reach their highest potential. How will you chart your course?

Chapter Four

Navigating Career Challenges and Change

We all aspire to have rewarding careers that offer fulfillment, impact, and financial security. Yet the path is rarely linear or predictable. While some enjoy steady progression up the corporate ladder before transitioning gracefully into retirement, others pinball chaotically between adventures and misadventures, with no shortage of wrong turns and dead ends along the way. Whether you prefer stability or thrive on change, building career resilience requires vigilance, adaptability, and a dose of luck.

When charting your career, the first fork in the road is whether you view it as a noun or a verb. If career is a noun, the end goal is a reliable progression to greater seniority and compensation over time before retiring. If career is a verb, it implies a more dynamic sequence of experiences, with less assurance of linear ascent but greater variety and excitement.

Of course, pure stability is largely a myth – disruptions happen. And unbridled careening eventually exacts a toll. The most resilient approach blends intentionality with flexibility, balancing some measure of planning for the future with openness to unexpected opportunities.

Long-term Career Strategy vs. Short-term Opportunities

Transforming our careers, launching new ventures, or guiding teams through transitions can seem enormously daunting. Yet pursuing bold dreams propels both personal and professional progress. Goal-setting helps convert initial fuzzy aspirations into concrete steps we can take today to manifest the futures we envision over time. Specifically, balancing long-term and short-term goals enables us to align daily tasks with the achievement of more ambitious endpoints. When wisely formulated and applied, such goals unleash our potential by channeling efforts toward what is meaningful and possible.

Clarifying Your Long-Term Trajectory

Long-term goals outline our desired achievements and evolution over an extended timeframe, often three years out or more. They inspire by depicting how we hope aspects of our life and work will take shape years down the line. For example, you may describe a future career transitioning from engineering into product management, launching a hospitality startup after next year, or relocating your growing company to a tech hub city after current projects conclude.

The aim is not to predict or control every detail of the future. Unexpected events and opportunities will inevitably reshape trajectories. However, defining long-term goals grants several advantages:

Purpose - A vivid portrait of your envisioned future provides direction, motivates ongoing efforts, and guides decision-making.

Expanded Possibilities - Breakthrough goals shake us from status quo thinking to consider bolder ambitions than we might otherwise pursue.

Confidence - As we make choices aligning near-term actions with long-term aspirations, self-trust and decisiveness increase.

Long-term goal-setting outlines a destination we believe worthy of sustained effort over years. Though the precise path there may meander, long-term goals enable progress.

Activating Your Vision with Short-Term Goals

If long-term goals describe desired endpoints years down the road, short-term goal-setting identifies milestones along the way. Short-term goals should advance your long-term aspirations while being achievable in days, weeks, or months. Revisiting the previous examples:

- You might enroll in a few product management courses this year (short-term) to enable a career transition next year (long-term).

- Before launching a hospitality startup, you could gain experience by operating a pop-up venue (short-term) that validates your model at small scale.

- Prior to relocation, current projects should establish self-sufficient teams and knowledge transfer protocols (short-term) to sustain operations when you decamp.

To maximize effectiveness, short-term goals should adhere to "SMART" principles. That means each short-term goal should be:

Specific - Clearly defined stepping stones.
Measurable - With tangible metrics or deliverables to track progress.
Achievable - Within current resource capacity and constraints.
Relevant - Aligning with long-term vision and priorities
Time-Bound - With a defined completion date.

Routinely assessing short-term goal achievement provides three main benefits:

1. Motivation - Short-term wins build momentum and buoy persistence toward bigger aims.

2. Feedback - Frequent checkpoints confirm you are on track or signal needed course corrections.

3. Agility - As circumstances evolve, short-term goals easily adjust to maintain alignment with overarching vision.

Short-term goal-setting translates ambitious long-term aspirations into executable near-term actions driving enduring change.

Maximum impact and fulfillment come from pursuing visions that beckon from the distant horizon yet translate into steps taken today. Long-term goals empower by reminding us of abiding purposes and possibilities. Short-term goals propel by channeling emerging potentials into defined incremental achievements. Together they enable progress.

When you feel overwhelmed consider this - the grandeur ahead is attained through focusing what is right in front of you now. Plot your coordinates toward the future. Then start ticking off your short-term goals that steadily take you there.

Avoiding Detours and Dead Ends

While personal agency alone does not dictate career trajectories, certain choices incline one toward resilience or roadblocks. This paper explores common pitfalls to sidestep in charting a purposeful professional path, framed within organizational, assignment-based, and interpersonal dynamics. Through diligent evaluation and strategic maneuvering, leaders can circumvent hindrances and maintain momentum on their journeys.

Joining the Wrong Organization

Selecting the right organizational home can make or break careers and enable or constrain success. When evaluating prospective employers, probe beneath the glossy recruiter pitches to objectively assess fundamentals: Is the organization built for growth or decline? Do capabilities match emerging market needs? Cultural cohesion and leadership impact also weigh heavily. While past accomplishments indicate potential, disruptive upheavals continually reshape industries and shuffle corporate fortunes. Flexibility to pivot as circumstances warrant pays dividends over time. Ultimately you must gauge alignment to your talents, interests and values beyond chasing arbitrary prestige.

Assessing Organizational Trajectories

Rapid expansion indicates a company has hit market fit and built internal capabilities to capitalize on opportunities. Leadership has effectively aligned strategy, structure, processes, and talent to growth demands. Consequently, rising organizations generally confer more advancement runway as they add roles and scope.

However, meteoric success one decade portends little about sustainability the next, given frequent disruptive threats. Like a meteoric rock, today's high-fliers may crash and burn into oblivion just as quickly.

Consider erstwhile category leaders in technology like Yahoo, desktop software titans like Lotus, or video rental chains like Blockbuster. At their apex, joining these dominators seemed like a sure path to prosperity. Yet each declined rapidly into irrelevance or extinction as internet search, mobile computing and streaming video eliminated strongholds.

Had you joined a telecommunications monopoly in the 1980s banking on their formidable market standing, you would have missed out on far greater opportunities in the emergent mobile phone sector. The bureaucratic old guards fixated on preserving legacy were blindsided by rapid change.

In contrast, those joining the right upstarts in their formative years reaped outsized rewards as new marketstook off. Early hires in companies like Google, Facebook, AirBnB, Tesla or Snowflake rode explosive growth trajectories most incumbent organizations only dream of matching.

Targeting Organizational Alignment

More than size or past success, lasting resonance requires ongoing alignment to market demands, capabilities that evolve intelligently as environments shift, and cultural cohesion that transcends transient challenges.

Thus when evaluating employers, scrutinize whether leadership grasps disruptive change underway and are making savvy bets on the future. Review how they develop talent and if you see room to stretch your capabilities in promising directions.

And observe cultural health, which no publicity campaign conveys accurately. Talk to employees at all levels to assess morale, trust in leadership, and cohesion around shared mission and values. Pervasive disconnects indicate dysfunction thwarting agility when crises hit.

No organization is immune to upheaval. But some build resilient capacity for reinvention rather than collapsing when traditional models falter. Seek out these enlightened organizations aiming not just to excel today but also to lead into the future.

And remain open to sometimes painful signals that once ideal jobs have soured. Have the courage to periodically reevaluate alignment amidst inevitability shifting individual and organizational trajectories over time.

Choose employers poised for market resonance and cultural cohesion over status. Commit to continual learning and evolution as industries transform. With discerning vision and flexibility, you can land in the right place as springboards for long-term success appear.

Chasing the Wrong Assignments

When evaluating potential assignments, probe beyond surface appearances. Aspiring leaders must discern undertakings positioned for relevance and resourcing from those doomed to flounder. Impactful assignments address systemic issues, secure executive sponsorship, and play to one's strengths. Additionally, visibility with decision-makers enables influence and advancement. Without such discernment, even technically sound work sinks into obscurity, benefiting no one while stifling careers.

Addressing Root Causes

Some assignments merely apply bandages to recurring problems without resolving underlying issues. You may successfully hit prescribed targets only to see problems resurface later.

For example, a client services team continuously scrambles to placate upset customers. However, frustrations trace back to gaps in product capabilities IT continually struggles to fulfill. Until root defects get prioritized, temporary salves will prove futile.

Before committing limited resources, assess if a proposal targets surface turmoil or core dysfunctions. Deficiencies may require process redesigns, system enhancements, or realigned budgets and accountability. Push sponsors to confront fundamental stabilizers. Otherwise, tread carefully into tenuous endeavors with minimal lasting impact.

Vetting Leadership Backing

Even initiatives addressing systemic deficits risk foundering without executive commitment. Those holding purse strings and influencing resourcing must buy into recommended interventions for success. So discern genuine interest up the chain of command.

Ask sharp questions - is leadership willing to rearrange budgets or processes to facilitate adoption? Can they eliminate obstacles likely to arise? Where will this rank amidst other priorities? Lackluster reassurances signal fading attention spans from those empowered to clear the path.

If convincing power brokers looks dicey, awaiting a riper opportunity may prove wise. Even the best ideas fail when starved of resources or throttled by entrenched interests protecting turf. Secure alignment before proceeding.

Playing to Strengths

Ensure proposed work aligns with your competencies and aspirations. No one excels at everything equally. Attempting assignments mismatches talents or interests with needs courts frustration.

For example, an extroverted visionary asked to meticulously audit financial records will likely chafe. Conversely, a meticulous analyst may struggle when asked to inspire change in ambiguous situations. Review skills demanded and assess fit.

Visibility Enables Impact

Beyond characteristics of the work itself, consider visibility with influencers. Contributions become forgotten, along with those making them, when removed from strategic priorities. Maintaining proximity to key decision makers enables influence.

Discerning promising assignments from those destined to disappoint requires perspective and wisdom. But efforts invested upfront assessing conditions for relevance and backing prevent pains later of canceled initiatives after significant sunk costs. Channel energies where able to create lasting value.

Mitigating Toxic Leadership

Leaders profoundly influence team engagement, performance, and advancement trajectories. But chemistry and compatibility vary. Overbearing authoritarians chase rapid turnover; lacking emotional intelligence, they interpret dissent as disloyalty. Conversely, empowering leaders develop through coaching and inspiration. When saddled with dysfunctional bosses, mitigating damage becomes key. If differences seem irreparable, discreetly seeking reassignment can be wise. If stuck, manage expectations carefully while expanding visibility with others. Maintain composure always - avoid emotional outbursts that exacerbate matters.

Evaluating Boss Compatibility

Take an honest inventory of your values and work styles. Do you require overt praise to stay motivated or prefer autonomous goal-setting? Are you comfortable with ambiguity or do you need detailed planning? What communication cadences enable trust?

Now objectively assess your boss's preferences. Does their leadership approach resonate or chronically chafe? Personality mismatches occur, but self-awareness minimizes friction.

Beware overbearing authoritarians who interpret dissent as disloyalty and compliance as the price of acceptance. Their boss-knows-best attitudes rarely foster collaborative cultures where talent thrives. If you require autonomy or influence over decisions affecting your work, resentment may fester.

Seeking Healthier Environments

When differences seem irreconcilable, discreetly explore reassignment options. Even lateral moves to more supportive leaders can reinvigorate. But avoid openly critiquing current superiors or declaring your intentions to leave prematurely. Word spreads quickly, jeopardizing references.

If unable to exit immediately, thoughtfully navigate expectations while expanding visibility with others. Communicate successes through department channels to pique interest for future collaborations. And remain composed publicly - emotional confrontations exacerbate matters.

Managing Expectations

When stuck with overbearing bosses, thoughtfully negotiate needs. Seek common ground and illuminate projects aligning to priorities. Frame requests around benefiting collective outcomes, not just personal preferences.

And anticipate reactions to adjust tactics accordingly. Hyperbolic bosses require extra validation to avoid knee-jerk criticism. Easily threatened bosses may bristle at unfiltered input. Adapting approaches smooths relations until able to transition to healthier alliances.

Preserving Confidence and Momentum

Toxic environments tax even highly skilled professionals. Counter draining cultures by taking inventory of accomplishments. Celebrate progress made despite challenges while strengthening supportive connections. Sustain momentum for the sake of the work itself and those you lead.

The more leadership assumes responsibility for developing talent, the less talent they retain. But with emotional intelligence and discretion, you can mitigate fallout. Nurture self-trust as you expand possibilities.

Incompatibility damages productivity and morale. But self-awareness, discretion, and adaptability prevent bad fits from derailing you completely. Seek environments enabling growth, but when trapped, judiciously mitigate.

Professional Ethics as the Foundation for Career Advancement

In a results-driven business culture fixated on outcomes, leaders often face pressure to compromise integrity to get ahead. Yet expedient rationalizations for unethical behavior inevitably carry lasting consequences that stunt careers rather than propel them upwards. Conversely, consistently modeling virtue accrues compounding dividends over time. When faced with murky dilemmas, the truest path for advancement lies through clarifying purpose, fortifying relationships, and focusing on genuine value creation.

Cultivating Character and Trust

In every interaction, we shape perceptions of our character either consciously or inadvertently. Over time, integrity displayed through adversity and temptation earns colleagues' trust far more than accomplishments alone. Such trust becomes the relational currency enabling career acceleration.

Consider two professionals with equal technical competencies being evaluated for a significant promotion. One has repeatedly kept commitments to teammates despite personal sacrifice and given credit to others' contributions every step of the way. Another has occasionally exaggerated claims of progress to impress executives and shifted blame during crises. All else being equal, who gets the nod? Undoubtedly the former, as character reputations directly impact mobility.

The Hyper-Connected Business Ecosystem

Unlike the past when disconnected organizationsopacity masked unscrupulous deeds, today's hyper-connected business ecosystems rapidly expose leaders' true colors. Unethical decisions detonate viral fallout destroying hard-won reputations instantaneously.

And damaged credibility proves nearly impossible to rebuild in communities wired to immediately distrust hints of scandal. See how quickly influencers forfeit public cachet when exposed for fabricating biographical details or buying artificial following counts. Yet leaders maintaining genuine transparency accrue exponential trust over decades through consistency.

When Ladders Slip

The Faustian bargain of sacrificing ethics for elevation promises fleeting gains followed by precipitous falls. Those cutting corners or compromising values to climb ladders soon grasp rotten rungs. They depend on silencing whistleblowers and preventing scrutiny to mask malfeasance. But suppression breeds fear and distrust rather than inspiration, undermining the talent and relationships on which leaders depend.

Meanwhile, the unethical leader grows isolated atop a crumbling pedestal, spending vital energy obscuring rather than pursuing higher aims. As cracks appear, desperation fuels increasingly brazen violations, culminating inevitably in explosions raining rubble on all below.

Building on Bedrock

Lasting success relies on cementing reputations and relationships on unshakeable foundations of trust established through recurring displays of integrity. When facing daunting obstacles, character shines as leaders elevate collective interests above selfish aims. Their resilient influence lifts others through crises.

While ethical leaders attract cohorts galvanized around shared values, transactional climbers surround themselves with convenient allies bought through favors quickly forgotten when fortunes shift.

Choose the path of principle in all you pursue. Reward will compound beyond trophies gathered or wealth accumulated. Lay worthy bricks day by day.

Some sacrifice virtue imagining momentary gain only to lose everything of abiding value, including self-respect. Build instead on bedrock by embedding ethics into all endeavors. Though the climb requires patience and care, the view from on high reveals horizons clear and welcoming.

Balancing Ambition with Teamwork

Organizations need both ambitious go-getters and great teamwork to thrive. Driven high-achievers pursue big goals. But they need collaborative teammates too. Go-getting energy must be directed toward group efforts, not undermine them. With thoughtful leadership, personal ambitions and shared success can fuel each other.

How Collaborating Accelerates Individual Growth

Research confirms that collaborating accelerates learning and skills (Grant & Berry, 2011). Ambitious professionals grow faster when they team up. Working together exposes them to new ideas and best practices. Accountability to teammates also stretches people to try unfamiliar roles. So collaboration provides a training gym for ambition.

Additionally, solving problems as a team inspires creative solutions. Different viewpoints trigger breakthrough concepts. An idea one person proposes may get expanded by others' contributions. Soon fresh innovations emerge that no individual would have developed alone.

Overall collaboration builds skills and confidence so ambitious folks can pursue bigger goals. Surrounded by those we respect, we feel pushed to match their example. It inspires bringing our A-game.

How Inner Drive Fuels Ambition

Inner drive is ambition's true fuel (Judge et al., 2005). Self-motivated high achievers aim for stretch targets and work relentlessly toward them. Their deep personal commitment keeps them practicing to master skills. It drives them to better their best. They feel fulfilled tackling huge challenges independently.

When ambitious people direct their own goals, their commitment intensifies. Chasing someone else's targets may incentivize temporary effort. But wanting goals ourselves makes us far more determined to power through obstacles.

Setbacks discourage those complying with handed-down goals yet energize the internally driven.

In summary, inner firestarters who set their own ambitious agendas often out-perform peers. Their self-created targets unlock maximum motivation.

Aligning Individual and Team Aims

Organizations must balance encouraging ambitious agency with directing it toward shared objectives so that person goals support collective success. Following practices help leaders and cultures achieve this synergy:

Connect to Common Purpose: Highlight how applying personal strengths to group goals significantly moves important shared priorities forward. This focuses individual ambitions on making broad positive impacts.

Promote Open Sharing: Create frequent forums for candid idea exchange and developmental feedback. Leaders should model transparency and contribution without fear of judgment. Soon sincere dialogue flows freely at all levels.

Spotlight Collaborative Achievements: Consistently recognize breakthrough results from team efforts. Praise collaborative problem-solving and creativity. When people feel valued for assisting teammates, bonds strengthen collaborative movement.

Demonstrate Balanced Partnership: Executives should exemplify interdependency between personal contributions and organization advancement. Listening before deciding and sharing credit builds trust in leadership commitment to partnership.

Enable Aligned Development: Provide growth opportunities elevating strengths directly applicable to strategic needs. This concurrently grows team capabilities while letting high-achievers build expertise in domains meaningful to them.

Organizational progress relies on focusing ambitious soloists' energies toward shared aims. Team alignment empowers exceptional individuals to amplify strengths. Great leadership awakens realization that no ambition finds complete fulfillment in isolation from collaborative enterprises. Progress unlocks when organizations effectively direct individuals' goals toward group success.

Key Takeaways & Final Thoughts on Navigating Career Challenges and Change

Key Takeaways:

- Collaboration amplifies skills-building and knowledge exchange, accelerating individual growth

- Inner drive and freedom to set ambitious personal targets maximize motivation and performance

- Aligning individual ambitions to collective purpose and shared accountabilities enables synergies between stars and constellations

Mobilizing Passions toward Shared Aspirations

Ambition provides potent fuel for achievement yet easily conflagrates into self-interest that fragments teams. Therefore, clarifying purpose proves essential to properly framing your calling within a broader mission. What talents and passions make you feel alive? How might dedicating these toward advancing collective goals make positive ripples? Leadership means elevating all boats, not jumping ahead alone.

Research confirms that collaborating exposes professionals to mental models expanding perspectives while accountability to respected colleagues urges crossing into unfamiliar growth territories (Grant & Berry, 2011). We lift our games when surrounded by those we admire. Seek assignments allowing reciprocal amplification of ambition with allies equally committed to excellence and shared ideals.

But also set aside alone-time for setting audacious personal targets beyond current capabilities. Innate drive provides the rocket fuel urging persistent improvement (Judge et al., 2005). Stretch goals typed up by others may incentivize temporary diligence but rarely spark enduring grit to surmount obstacles. Progress relies on internalizing objectives until they become profound personal priorities.

With so many competing priorities, ambivalent organizations unconsciously drift from espoused values. Promising initiatives flounder from under-investment; technical contributors hit dead-ends lacking leadership training. Amidst organizational chaos, defining your calling requires regularly realigning efforts to match espoused principles or collaborating to reshape reality toward truer north.

Stay attentive to small signals revealing cultural straying from ideal trajectories. Whether passed over repeatedly despite evident qualifications or observing inequities in access to opportunities, note discrepancies between words and actions. Then courageously advocate adjustments or lead boldly toward imagined alternatives.

Progress relies on internal accountability. How do my daily efforts strengthen others and move the needle on issues I care about? What wisdom do I still need to cultivate? An ambitious calling interweaves your unique abilities, values and priorities with the world's profound needs. When organizations fail to steward talents well, perhaps channels outside hierarchical confines offer fuller expression of purpose. The more clarity gained, the more confidently you can align ambitions with the greater good.

Chapter Five

Strategies for Leadership Promotion

Getting promoted to a leadership role takes more than just hard work and strong performance. Even dedicated employees with years of service can find themselves stuck or overlooked when promotion opportunities arise. However, with the right strategies and mindset, professionals at any level can increase their chances to advance into leadership. This guide examines common promotion pitfalls, essential visibility tactics, and the proactive yet patient approach necessary to ascend the ranks with resilience.

At first glance, the path upwards seems straightforward - work hard, meet targets, demonstrate capability. But the reality of corporate advancement rarely aligns with such an idealistic formula. Exceptional individual contributors do not automatically get tapped for leadership; in fact, plenty of mediocre managers secured promotions through office politics, self-promotion, or simply being in the right place at the right time.

Rather than resign yourself to bitterness or helplessness, reshape your career strategy using research-backed methods. A seminal study by leadership expert

Herminia Ibarra found active relationship building to be the #1 tactic used by professionals who made successful transitions into senior roles. Meanwhile, Columbia Business School Professor Joel Brockner's findings on organizational justice indicate that employees need to perceive fairness in promotion criteria rather than seeing advancement as a black box process. Equipped with such insights, you can proactively yet strategically position yourself for leadership.

Scrutinize Structural Shortcomings

The first step involves an honest personal assessment about your position within the company structure. Ask yourself these key questions:

Do I have the right role and manager to gain exposure?

Entry-level jobs and controlling managers rarely set up employees for visibility. Seek lateral moves into roles where you can demonstrate competencies required at the next level, such as managing complex projects, overseeing teams, and interacting cross-functionally.

Have I actively sought feedback about advancement?

You cannot reasonably expect a promotion if you never express interest or discuss your prospects with decision-makers. Have transparent, solutions-oriented conversations about growth opportunities with your manager. Identify skill gaps holding you back so you can proactively address them.

Does my work align with organization values and culture?

The right technical expertise only gets you so far. Your interpersonal behaviors, communication style, and cultural fit also influence promotion readiness. Observe how leaders embody company values; emulate role models who align with the formal and informal norms.

Increase Visibility Systematically

With a supportive reporting structure in place, you can implement tactical solutions to increase visibility, starting with these best practices:

Leverage big projects strategically.

When high-profile initiatives arise, raise your hand to get involved even if the extra work seems daunting. Stretch yourself to demonstrate leadership potential. Gain familiarity with directors and VPs overseeing the key deliverables.

Present to senior stakeholders.

Prepare thoroughly to make a stellar impression when given the opportunity to present to executive teams or external clients. Seek feedback afterwards; implement advice to polish your communications style. Follow up on concerns, building stakeholder relationships.

Network beyond your immediate team.

Avoid career silos by introducing yourself more widely across departments, building both peer relationships and executive connections. Follow influential leaders on company channels; engage professionally with their content. Look for mentors who can advise you.

Earn referrals through consistent excellence.

Day-to-day, maximize performance and helpfulness without compromise. When leaders encounter challenges needing expert support, your name should quickly come to mind thanks to your solid reputation.

Develop Patient Persistence

With advanced qualifications, tactical visibility, and a results-driven work ethic in place, you may expect instant gratification in the form of a promotion. But the nature of large organizations necessitates patience through the advancement process. Mistakes like the following can impede your progress:

- Pushing aggressively for promotion every review cycle – This approach causes resentment rather than results.

- Overwhelming executives as you blindly volunteer for every project – Be strategic with your time and availability.

- Gossiping or complaining about passed over promotions – Maintain integrity even in disappointment.

- Threatening to quit unless promoted – It backfires by depicting you as disloyal.

Instead, manifest calm determination in these ways:

- Commit to six more months when passed over – Regroup and build your case with good humor.

- Request candid feedback about readiness – Listen earnestly, then implement improvement plans.

- Celebrate colleague promotions genuinely – Foster goodwill; support transitions cooperatively.

- Trust your growth trajectory – Each year adds experience; believe leadership awaits in due course.

With structured planning, persistent networking, and values alignment, leaders often emerge where least expected. Follow this advice to build your reputation as an indispensable contributor. Streamline your priorities rather than getting overwhelmed. Growth into leadership requires planting seeds patiently – then enjoying the fruits of resilience when you get tapped at just the right time.

Avoiding Missteps on the Path to Leadership

Seeking promotions while maintaining ethical standards presents dilemmas at every turn. However ambitious employees may fix their sights on the next opportunity, practical realities often fail to align with such aspirations of advancement. Corporate hierarchies brim with intricate social networks and political landmines. Even diligent workers with impeccable qualifications cannot control every external factor impacting their upward mobility. Recognizing common mistakes made in pursuing promotions empowers professionals to navigate potential pitfalls with integrity.

What Promotion Seekers Get Wrong

Employees frequently torpedo their own advancement by overestimating meritocracy. The notion that exceptional individual performance leads directly to recognition propels many eager go-getters attempting to climb the corporate ladder quickly through pure hard work and skill mastery alone. Such aggressive efforts inevitably expose inexperience about the true nuances of organizational culture.

Well-intentioned attempts to display dedication frequently backfire due to lack of alignment with unwritten expectations around acceptable self-promotion. Candidates concentrating solely on assignments may miss cues about broader organizational priorities and informal processes influencing hiring decisions. Rather than relying on assumptions, professionals seeking elevation must balance tactical visibility pursuits with un arrogant patience about timing.

Problematic Patterns in Seeking Advancement

Certain behaviors and conversations around promotions routinely undermine an employee's credibility despite good intentions behind the efforts. Common problematic patterns include:

- Pressuring leaders repetitively about promotions or compensation during every review cycle. Such naked ambition scans as entitled or out of touch.

- Overwhelming directors with overly eager volunteering without context about bandwidth. The passion appears misguided rather than strategic.

- Gossiping with colleagues about being passed over for advancement. The negativity smells of resentment rather than readiness.

- Threatening departure unless receiving a promotion. The disloyalty reveals ulterior motives over serving the organization.

- Complaining about leadership hiring externally to fill roles. The presumption comes across as arrogant and unjustified.

- Highlighting competitors' offers to force negotiations. The strong-arm tactics rupture trust and goodwill.

In each case, professionals contradict their own abilities by reaching too far, too fast without relationship context to ground the overtures. However technically capable an employee may be, such interpersonal fumbles undermine leadership potential. Seekers must self-reflect on alignment between personal values and organizational culture before pushing advancement conversations.

Strategic Positioning: The Balancing Act

True leaders advance by balancing tactical visibility with patient humility. This means performing excellently at current responsibilities while strategic positioning for growth by:

- Establishing visibility across departments through networking.

- Seeking high-impact stretch assignments to demonstrate strengths.

- Presenting confidently when interfacing with executives.

- Consistently exceeding expectations in existing role responsibilities.

Simultaneously, it also involves waiting gracefully by:

- Avoiding confrontation even when passed over initially.

- Embracing opportunities thatelevate colleagues.

- Keeping long term career fulfillment as the ultimate prize over title chasing.

- Trusting that sustained performance gets rewarded in due time by those who notice.

This balancing act proves challenging but serves the organization's interests first and foremost. Leaders adopt abundance mindsets with faith that recognized excellence inevitably ascends rank not according to artificial timelines but emergent need.

Executive Awareness: Cultural Alignment

Since influence accrues to those highly attuned to unwritten expectations, aspiring executives must observe nuanced dynamics. Powerful gatekeepers prioritize team players enculturated with values over skills alone. Common criteria include:

How consistently an employee's behaviors reinforce guiding principles. Cultural fit indicates fundamental alignment that facilitates trust in high pressure situations. Leaders seek to mitigate risks in advancement decisions by choosing known entities.

Whether existing managers advocate for the promotion. Internal referrals hold credibility since familiarity allows realistic assessment of work ethic and temperament. Outsider observers possess limited context. So a lukewarm endorsement from an immediate supervisor severely damages a candidate's credibility.

What interpersonal impacts the employee has organization-wide. Leaders want collaborators with solid reputations across functions who earn respect where the formal powers of title cannot exert direct control. A strong internal brand earns the benefit of the doubt during advancement considerations.

The context around business needs directing hiring decisions. Opening arise not from abstract criteria but embedded realities around budgets, talent availability, project pipelines. Rather than taking outcomes personally, optimistic persistence pays dividends.

By mastering essential responsibilities while demonstrating authentic cultural fit, aspiring executives play the long game in career advancement. Prioritizing relationship building and values alignment over rushing the process earns respect from established gatekeepers. With intentional positioning, leaders often emerge from unexpected spaces. The key becomes planting seeds generously without fixating on inevitable harvests.

Assessing Organizational Fit

We spend over 90,000 hours at work over a lifetime. Yet many professionals overlook company culture while chasing job offers, only to discover values misalignment after joining organizations and teams. But culture directly impacts engagement, performance, and retention. Savvy job seekers can now assess critical soft factors influencing workplace satisfaction using insider perspectives shared openly through digital channels. By complementing traditional hiring conversations with crowdsourced worker feedback, candidates enter new roles with eyes wide open about cultural dynamics shaping their employee experience.

Leaders recognize that aligned culture drives business success. Consider how Enron's toxic culture rooted in fear and greed fueled financial disasters. Meanwhile, Netflix's freedom and responsibility culture catalyzes innovation and growth. But companies struggle to impart cultural facets during short courtship periods. Recruiters sell dreams while candidates sell competence. Deep culture comprehension eludes both parties. Yet proactive individuals can pierce through the conventional hiring facade using foresight.

Researching Culture from the Outside

Substantial cultural clues hide in plain sight across an organization's digital footprint for those willing to devote sleuthing efforts. Every company projects images reflecting internal realities through websites, job postings, blog posts and social media. Review these sources critically not just as a potential employee but also as a customer assessing the brand's trustworthiness in representing values.

The archetypal mission statement should encapsulate guiding philosophies. But cookie-cutter corporate jargon like "innovative excellence" rings empty without context. Analyze if executive messaging and market positioning align with slogans. For example, does a company boasting ethics actively address recent scandals through leadership communiques or whistleblower policies?

Furthermore, an engaging cross-functional company blog with transparent storytelling suggests open flows of communication. Contrarily, an arid newsroom populated only by public relations talking points reveals shallow employee access. Explore these vital signs before believing wellness platitudes.

Surveys deliver the most unvarnished views direct from those toiling within organizations unseen by recruiters. Sites like Glassdoor and Indeed centralize employee feedback about culture with well-designed interfaces for investigating specific companies. Here candid reviewers anonymously critique leadership, collaboration dynamics, advancement potential and perks. While considering grain of salt skepticism around disgruntled outlier perspectives, highly consistent employee sentiments warrant thoughtful reflection, especially if alignment with your priorities lacks.

Discussing Culture During Interviews

Once research provides baseline perceptions, hiring conversations allow exploration of nuanced questions personalized for your preferences. But forearmed candidates often neglect to ask culture queries, instead fielding imagined "right answers" to impress. Fight this instinct by directing dialogue towards topics revealing whether your working style and values thrive within existing environments.

Consider asking interviewers why they commit time specifically to this organization rather than chasing paychecks elsewhere. Authentic answers disclosing affinity expose purpose, leadership and camaraderie. Even small cultural pivot anecdotes prove enlightening, like how teams rallied during pandemic cutbacks or how dissent gets voiced constructively. Listen for fulfillment or robotic disengagement.

Additionally discussany rhythms suggesting lively cultures, from ideation meetings to relief valves like office outings or digital watercooler chat apps. Does ubiquitous collaboration software meet genuine connection needs? Explore policies around remote work flexibility or parental leave signalling investment in whole self well-being. Probe how ethical concerns raised by employees receive addressing. Thoughtful questioning unveils vital intangibles.

Observing Interpersonal Cultural Indicators

Look beyond verbal exchanges alone when discerning culture fit. Consider micro-behaviors, environmental vibesand intuition during hiring engagements for insights. Do phone screeners exhibit active listening and empathy or box-checking apathy? Such early interactions establish cultural expectations around respect. Attentive recruiting experiences portend psychologically safe workplaces where speaking up won't get you branded as "not a team player."

Upon visiting offices, blend both clinical and emotional observations when touring spaces, watching interactions and visual environmental clues reflecting values. Are physical surroundings freshly modernized or dated in design? How do front-line staff great guests checking in? When passing other areas, do you witness laughter signalling morale and camaraderie? Such seemingly trivial aspects coalesce around overall culture health.

During interviews themselves note how conversations flow. Do panelists collaborate to answer questions or rigidly adhere to functional silos in isolation? Does the group reflect diverse perspectives and backgrounds? Scan for signs of belonging through displayed personal artifacts like family photos against the contrasts of sterile cubicles signalling disengagement. Follow subtle emotional responses to your questions as well. Places where you can envision flourishing spark positive energy, whereas toxic workplaces afflict anxiety.

Confirming Alignment Deliberately

Undoubtedly, culture lives within unspoken realms challenging to discern as an outsider. But thoughtfully approaching hiring engagements by complementing standard procedures with added discernment tactics empowers stronger career decisions. Wield insider perspectives collected from current employees, leveraging research ahead of time rather than relying on recruiter rhetoric alone. Ask meaningful culture questions, observing interpersonal dynamics simultaneously. Ultimately trust both reason and instinct during crucial alignment audits preceding commitment. You will work alongside these people fulfilling or draining your spirit soon enough. Choose workplaces wisely where you know culture matters, however ineffable the ingredients.

Key Takeaways & Final Thoughts on Strategies for Leadership Promotion

Key Takeaways:

- Seeking promotions requires balancing visible achievements with patient timing while demonstrating cultural fit.

- Common missteps like aggressive self-promotion or entitlement undermine leadership potential despite technical capabilities.

- Strategic networking, high-impact volunteer projects and consistent performance signal readiness while avoiding problematic behaviors.

- Executives assess cultural alignment including peer advocacy, values embodiment and contextual business needs when considering advancement.

Pursuing Promotion Pathways with Authenticity

Navigating career ladders tests worker integrity at every rung. Impatient high achievers often self-sabotage advancement prospects through misguided tactics despite impressive credentials. Meanwhile, understated team players arise on executive radar through cultural synchronization. As this discussion illuminated, promotion processes hinge on far more than individual productivity for those with leadership aspirations. Securing elevations the right way matters just as much.

The impatient strivers and behind-the-scenes bloomers represent two archetypes seeking to climb corporate hierarchies. The former leans on accomplishment volumes, working furiously to compile visible wins by raising hands first and speaking loudest to showcase capability. But such transparent ambition scans as arrogance or entitlement that erodes cultural capital. Meanwhile, modest team players focus humbly on role excellence while strategically expanding associate networks. Trust accrues gradually to those accentuating positivity. When the timing aligns with business objectives, these understated in-group talents surface as promotion candidates. They embrace opportunities with gratitude rather than expectation. Both personality types can prove effective leaders but must temper tendencies with self-awareness around countersproductive behaviors that undermine credibility.

Rather than chasing promotions as an end unto itself, professionals should adopt sturdy ethical foundations while demonstrating readiness through consistent performance. This allows believable assimilation into elevated levels of authority and accountability. Leadership cannot be reduced to a formula. Those who inspire followers lead by empowering teams to drive outcomes rather than selfish interests. They embrace company growth with passion, navigating setbacks by rallying groups towards solutions. Every workforce needs servant leaders who check egos for the collective benefit. Promotion processes reveal who lives these qualities before roles expand scope. Be the change by lifting others.

What signals demonstrate genuine care beyond skills and strategy? How can professionals augment cultural connectivity during advancement pursuit? The answers require looking inward and outward simultaneously. Consider misalignment risks before overreaching. But also recognize where hungry teams need your full talents realized through earned leadership platforms. Then progress forwards confidently one aligned step after another.

Chapter Six

Career Crossroads: Deciding When to Move On

As a leader, there will come a point where you have to make a tough call: Should I stay in my current job or move to a new opportunity? Careers take unexpected turns, with good times and bad times. Reaching career goals involves getting through challenges, not just smooth sailing. Some leaders work through tough situations, before eventually realizing their career is stalled with no signs of progress. Knowing when to stick it out or make a change is crucial.

This decision requires honest reflection about yourself, evaluating if your current role sets you up for success, and thinking about future learning. If these elements show that progress seems unlikely in your current job, even though leaving brings uncertainty, moving on may be the best path forward. Let's explore how to approach this decision wisely.

Reflect on Your Strengths and Passions

First, reflect inward. What talents and interests motivate you? What work settings and tasks spur you to do your best? How do you personally define career success beyond status or money? These important questions show what matters most for job satisfaction based on your values.

This self-reflection prevents hastily quitting when issues emerge. Short-term problems differ from dead-end jobs. Knowing yourself helps differentiate temporary struggles from stalled careers lacking growth potential. Additionally, connecting to your passions powers resilience amid adversity when changing jobs feels uncertain. Defining success for yourself recharges your motivation to keep trying when formal success measures decline.

Take time for honest self-evaluation during career crossroads. Balance emotions using inner wisdom so you don't change jobs incorrectly or stay too long in an unsatisfying role unaware. Talk to mentors who understand your abilities best. Discuss options matching your capabilities and motivations. Once self-aware, examine if your current job enables success.

Evaluate if Your Job Enables Growth

When dissatisfied, investigate whether the issues are with your specific job or the organization. Seek facts over feelings. Is progress stalled temporarily or impossible long-term? Review past trends and future projections.

For instance, conflict with a manager could prove temporary if the organization is thriving with transfer options. However, toxicity infecting the whole company indicates deeper issues. Determine if challenges come from temporary external factors or worsening culture and incompetence.

Additionally, research upcoming changes like mergers, leadership shifts, or expansion plans that might improve or worsen conditions. Short-term struggles due to infrastructure upgrades differ greatly from irreparable systemic issues.

Evaluate your job fit too. Do you just need more support or complete responsibilities better suiting your capabilities? Distinguish between fixable resourcing problems versus role mismatches misaligning your strengths.

Carefully investigating root causes and projected outlooks informs wise decisions on whether to stay or move on.

Recognizing Stagnation in Your Career

We embark on our careers with aspirations of where we want to go and who we want to become. Yet along the journey, you will likely grapple with the feeling that you are losing momentum or even going nowhere. If this happens only once in your career, consider yourself fortunate.

With flexible work arrangements and employee leverage growing, our jobs increasingly intersect with our personal lives. More individuals at all career stages, from new entrants to veterans, are questioning aspects central to their work lives: What organization aligns to my values? What work is most meaningful? Who do I want to work with and how?

These soul-searching questions often signify stagnation, where you stop progressing. For ambitious professionals who thrive on growth, stagnation breeds deep discomfort. However, recognizing stagnation primes you to reignite engagement. By examining causes and signs of stagnation, as well as potential remedies, you can refresh professional fulfillment. Let's explore how to recapture momentum when your career stalls.

Defining Career Stagnation

Stagnation refers to lacking forward movement or development. Many define careers narrowly by titles and salaries. However, stagnation manifests more broadly when your day-to-day work lacks learning, autonomy, impact, or purpose. These intrinsic elements largely drive job satisfaction and performance.

Stagnation proves perfectly acceptable for some. Stability, predictability, and minimal change suit many. However, if you yearn for intense development, stagnation, however brief, causes concern.

High achievers stress about going nowhere not from mere restlessness, but because progress connects deeply to identity and self-worth. Stagnation signals losing competencies that make you stand out. It resembles being stuck on the sideline as others play the game. Furthermore, languishing in roles misaligned with your interests breeds resentment, not just impatience. Realizing your strengths and passions are muted rather than catalyzed at work seems like a betrayal.

Recognizing stagnation marks a pivotal first step to recharting your professional course. By identifying where momentum has faded and why, you can regain excitement about your contributions.

Common Signs Your Career is Stagnated

While no universal metric defines stagnation, several red flags signal waning engagement:

1. *Lack of Learning:* Stagnation often accompanies skill atrophy, where you repeat routine assignments without expanding capabilities. Perhaps you once eagerly awaited new techniques and domains. Now projects feel like reruns. You realize that your expertise plateaued long ago without consciously noticing.

2. *No Progression:* Another sign involves output exceeding outcomes. Despite dedicated efforts, your boss overlooks your accomplishments. Your responsibilities swell but titles and pay stay static. Once-ambitious goals now seem fantasies. This gap between effort and rewards breeds cynicism.

3. *Muted Passion:* As daily stimulation and challenge decline, passion fades. You log hours simply earning a living without purposeful im-

pact. Where work once energized you, now you watch the clock until quitting time. Passion's absence leaves a palpable void, emotionally and motivationally.

Each person's stagnation symptoms and tolerance levels differ. Comparing yourself against blanket benchmarks proves fruitless. Instead, tune into your unique needs and values to assess engagement. Then strategize solutions, starting with identifying what stalled your progress.

Top Causes of Career Stagnation

Stagnation results from individual decisions and organizational realities. The common causes include:

1. *Poor Cultural Fit:* Over time, the organization's values may diverge from your own. What once seemed an aligned culture shifts, or else you evolve. Perhaps innovation is rewarded in principle but not practice. Deeply engrained hierarchies thwart fresh thinking. Such divides breed disengagement over time.

2. *Blocked Opportunities:* Regardless of your competence and commitment, organizations may fail to reward your efforts and provide outlets for advancement. With no accountability for internal talent mobility, managerial bottlenecks prevent qualified candidates from accessing opportunities. Dead-end jobs offer few alternatives.

3. *Skills-Role Mismatch:* Stagnation also stems from organizations pigeonholing employees rather than enabling growth across diverse assignments. They reward stability over mobility. Even eager learners ossify if trapped doing the same task forever without space to stretch.

4. *Poor Leadership:* Disengaged leaders breed disengaged teams. If your manager ignores emerging capabilities or grasps tight onto status quo processes, your contributions are stifled. Leaders accountable for talent development beget energized professionals. The opposite remains

likewise true.

5. *Lack of Ownership:* Stagnation depends partly on the individual, not just the organization. You may passively expect opportunities to be handed rather than proactively crafting your role. Without voicing goals or volunteering for assignments, you drift along. Owning your growth path counteracts stagnation.

Resolutions Depend on Root Causes

Just as no single cause triggers stagnation uniformly, no one solution works universally. Remedies target specific stagnation drivers. However, certain strategies apply more broadly:

1. *Refresh Skills:* Combat skill atrophy by allotting time for learning. Devour books, articles, podcasts, and webinars to stay abreast of industry advancements. Sign up for courses introducing new competencies. Learn analytics, programming, communications, or whatever capabilities augment your role. Budgeting dedicated learning time builds momentum.

2. *Increase Visibility:* To address limited mobility, amplify visibility into your achievements and aspirations. When appropriate, detail successful initiatives in meetings with data demonstrating impact. Specify how projects align with company goals so leadership connects ideas to strategic value. Proactively request conversations with influencers about advancement.

3. *Voice Needs:* Rather than expecting managers to sense your disengagement, clearly communicate needs. Frame this as aiming to contribute more fully utilizing your skills, not just seeking self-gain. Suggest specific projects aligning individual and organizational interests. Bring solutions, not just problems. Enable win-win resolutions.

4. *Assess Alternatives:* When misfit with company culture or role leaves

few options internally, carefully evaluate external opportunities. But avoid reflexively quitting without purposefully progressing towards settings better suited to who you are and want to become. Consider if grass only seems greener elsewhere without watering your own lawn first.

5. *Owning Your Career:* Ultimately professionals stagnate when relinquishing agency over their careers and placing destiny in the organization's hands. Regaining momentum requires accepting responsibility as the driver of your development journey. This means periodically charting your course based on long-term goals, not just reacting when dissatisfied. Aimlessly floating makes you hostage to external currents. Proactively steering your ship prevents such drift.

Embrace Continuous Learning

Career changes understandably cause anxiety about the unknown. However, complacency in unfulfilling jobs poses greater risks than seeking new opportunities. Have courage to redirect when examination and facts show your current job is going nowhere. The right roles and supportive leadership make all the difference.

With a learning mindset, challenges become growth opportunities rather than threats. View yourself as an ever-developing leader gaining skills to succeed in diverse settings. Setbacks sometimes come from capability gaps, not incompetence. Be patient in building knowledge. Avoid comparing against others seemingly excelling. Instead, focus on self-improvement using each experience to enhance your abilities.

Choose supportive managers invested in developing staff while working towards organizational growth. Let them help you address skill gaps so you can confidently navigate workplace changes. Whether staying despite temporary barriers or discovering new possibilities, maintaining a learning mentality empowers you to progress through uncertainty.

Key Takeaways & Final Thoughts on Career Crossroads: Deciding When to Move On

Key Takeaways:

- Stagnation manifests when progress halts – lacking learning, advancement, passion, or purpose. Recognizing symptoms like skill atrophy, limited mobility, and eroding engagement prompts revitalization.

- Causes range from poor culture fit, blocked opportunities, skills-role mismatches, disengaged leadership, and failing to own your career. Resolutions depend on the roots.

- Strategies include reskilling, increased visibility, voicing needs assertively, assessing alternatives, and periodically recalibrating alignment with goals.

Owning Your Career Journey

Our career paths wind and bend in unexpected ways. What began as a steady climb can plateau unexpectedly. Or worse, the terrain turns treacherous, and we realize the path leads nowhere at all.

Facing such crossroads proves unsettling, even frightening. Do we stubbornly keep climbing a path growing ever steeper? Do we attempt to chart a new course amid the unknown? Every fiber of our being leans towards the familiar, resisting the risk that changing direction might leave us more lost than before.

And yet, nostalgia often clouds our judgment. We remember the exhilaration of progress but forget the creeping unease as momentum slowed. Signposts signaling danger ahead went unheeded until stagnation fully blocked our way.

Only by confronting hard truths can we walk the next mile: this path has ended. It is time to forge a new one.

The first step requires honesty to admit when stagnation sets in, though the symptoms can be subtle. Feelings of boredom, cynicism, or defeat displace passion and purpose. Skills wither without challenge or visibility shrinks despite dedicated efforts. Recognizing these signals promptly proves crucial, lest malaise hardens into despair.

Once acknowledged, seeking solutions also demands bravery. We must own that charter rather than idle passively at the crossroads. Reskilling, increased assertiveness and assessing options all play a role. But above all, lasting revitalization relies on periodically recalibrating our inner compass towards the true north of our talents and values. Only by facing this difficult reckoning can we walk ahead with courage and conviction instead of looking back longingly.

The course of careers never does run smooth. Stormy seasons lay ahead. But by embracing agency over our journeys, with wisdom and purpose rather than regret or resentment, we can navigate any crossroads. For in the end, it is not the terrain itself but the vision and vigor we bring to the trail that determines how far we travel in our careers.

Chapter Seven

Building Resilience for the Long Haul

The path to leadership has often been compared to running a marathon rather than a sprint. While leaders may experience bursts of progress along their journey, maintaining momentum requires pacing oneself for the long haul. This analogy highlights the need to cultivate resilience in order to effectively lead over the course of one's career. However, what specific strategies can rising leaders employ to sustain their drive while avoiding burnout? By examining some key lifestyle factors, establishing healthy boundaries, and finding purpose and enjoyment in one's work, individuals can equip themselves to thrive in leadership roles over decades of service.

Firstly, leaders must assess aspects of their health and wellbeing which impact resilience, carefully balancing intense effort with recovery. Studies show that consistently overworking leads to diminished returns in performance and creativity over time. While passion for meaningful work provides fuel for the race, exhaustion causes runners to stumble. Regularly clocking extreme hours every week, failing to take adequate vacation, and letting work obligations creep into personal life can all take their toll. Warning signs like constant tiredness, frequent illness, and lack of life balance indicate unsustainable patterns for the long-term leadership challenge. Just as sobriety benefits workplace productivity, adequate rest serves leaders better than proudly wearing fatigue as a badge of honor.

With self-awareness about these dynamics, individuals can take proactive steps to modulate lifestyle factors accordingly. Eating nutrient-rich whole foods provides better energy than convenience snacks over years of exertion. Identifying enjoyable forms of movement keeps circulation pumping when intensity might otherwise encourage sedentary shortcuts. Leaders should give themselves permission to cultivate interests outside work which spark inspiration, whether athletic pursuits, creative outlets, community bonds, or intellectual exploration. Carving out true disconnection from constant digital tethers offers space for reflection. While balance looks different for each person, the common thread involves honoring one's whole being, not just professional obligations.

This also means establishing appropriate boundaries around workload and workplace stressors. Researchers emphasize that pressure stems more from middle management rather than executive roles at the organizational helm. While senior leaders carry greater responsibility, they also gain authority to delegate tasks and shape cultural expectations. They have enough runway to bring considered strategy to high-stakes decisions. With perspective from life experience, they see business cycles ebb and flow. These factors empower leaders to work smarter, not just harder, as they steer collective objectives.

Rather than an excuse for laziness, work-life balance allows individuals to thrive in the marathon by mitigating burnout. Much like adequate sleep enhances workplace performance, quality downtime makes leaders better primed for the next sprint. Psychological detachment from constant urgency renews mental focus and emotional resilience. By modeling such boundaries, executives also give permission for employees to craft sustainable workflows as well. Work martyrdom helps no one in the long run. Savvy leaders demonstrate that whole health bolsters capacity to steer group progress over grueling courses stretching across vocational lifetimes.

Beyond self-care practices, a sense of purpose propels leaders through exhausting stretches of the journey. Passion for making a difference and leaving a meaningful legacy links today's efforts with tomorrow's impact. This sense of contribution toward things greater than oneself fuels inner reservoirs of determination decade after decade. Leaders driven purely by status or financial incentives often find such external markers ring hollow before reaching the finish line. Intrinsic motivations stand the test of time.

Fortunately, research on senior management repeatedly reveals that such leaders authentically enjoy their vocational callings. Unlike middle managers immersed in organizational minutiae, chief executives keep their sights trained on the horizons ahead. Making high-stakes decisions proves exhilarating, not burdensome, for those who stepped forward to guide collective potential. Executives inhabit roles matching their strengths and convictions after many years of self-discovery in the leadership arena. With childlike wonder rather than resentful obligation, such leaders wake excited to take on new challenges which push their capabilities. Their lifelong dedication flows not from compulsion but passion.

For those earlier on the path, connecting work tasks to personal meaning makes the journey ahead more sustainable. Leaders clarify their values, interests, and priorities before committing to career trajectories spanning decades. Doing what one loves prevents waking up years later stuck on paths divergent from who one has become. Without enjoying the daily ground covered, travelers risk disillusionment in leadership roles. However, when vocational journeys align with authentic identity, the marathon course ahead feels like a scenic route rather than a dread treadmill.

Leadership calls for extraordinary endurance across the long haul. Executives carry responsibilities affecting countless lives for many years. But rather than barely surviving such journeys, leaders can equip themselves to thrive decade after decade through intentional resilience practices. Assessing lifestyle factors, establishing healthy boundaries, and connecting work to personal meaning all pave the way for sustaining passion through long-distance races. Leadership summons individuals to a lifelong commitment, not a halfhearted sprint. By caring for mental, emotional, physical and spiritual wellbeing along the road ahead, rising leaders prepare to stay the course with energy left to finish strong. Just like marathon training, consistency proves key - not just heroic efforts without recovery.

How to Maintain Motivation for the Long Haul

What drives someone to pursue a goal tirelessly for months or years? Motivation stems from internal motives that compel us toward something we desire. Unlike fleeting New Year's commitments to improve fitness or career prospects, long-term motivation is consciously chosen and repeatedly acted upon despite difficulty. By reflecting on our deepest hopes, connecting current tasks to larger purposes, focusing mental and physical energy toward continual progress, and maintaining a positive mindset, we can sustain motivation over time to achieve ambitious dreams.

Clarifying Purpose

Behind every long-term effort lies intention rooted in needs and desires. Sustained motivation flows from consciously clarifying why a goal matters and how achieving it will fulfill personal longing or benefit others. Individuals who reflect deeply on their motives choose pursuits aligned with inner purpose rather than defaulting to societal scripts.

For instance, the decision to train for a marathon requires envisioning the future accomplishment and how it satisfies intrinsic yearnings for challenge or community connection. Every early morning run in the dark and late night stretching session links to that clarified intention; the immediate choice energizes the ultimate aim. Without a purposeful motive that resonates at one's core, motivation relies on sheer discipline. But with a meaningful intention, dedication flows more naturally through seasons of difficulty.

Connecting today's tasks, however mundane, to a future vision channels energy into each small step. Even repetitive actions gain significance since they pave the way for dramatic change. Purpose fuels passionate and sustained effort not through demanding gritted teeth but by repeatedly choosing what matters most.

Executing with Discipline

et even the loftiest motivations require channeling inspiration into consistent execution. Long-term goals demand relentless discipline applied to incremental gains. Sustaining effort day after day, especially when progress stalls or boredom sets in, differentiates fleeting bursts from lifelong trajectories.

Say an individual feels called to leadership influence that improves lives. Beyond enrolling in graduate seminars, they must also digest dense texts on weekends when friends gather for fun. They relinquish promotions that provide more income but limit leadership opportunities. In rainy predawn hours, they compose written proposals for innovative projects when the comfort of sleep beckons. Each disciplined investment flows from the initial sense of purpose; together they build capability to match motivation.

This execution with focused intent continues during seasons when visible outcomes lag. Motivated leaders submit funding applications for their initiatives month after month, undaunted by initial rejections. Scientists repeat failed experiments hunting for elusive breakthroughs over entire careers. Disciplined effort powers progress behind the scenes until sudden visible results surprise everyone except those motivated for the long haul.

Maintaining Energy

Executing with discipline over decades requires regularly renewing physical, mental and emotional energy. Otherwise fatigue undermines sustained effort as motivation stalls. High achievers build rhythms of effort and recovery into crowded calendars.

Intense work periods incentivize leaders to then unwind fully rather than half-heartedly distracting themselves with screens. Guarding sleep cycles enables waking energy for maximum contribution rather than chronic depletion. Exercise and healthy nutrition empower endurance like training regimens for marathoners. Breaks should provide complete detachment from occupational concerns rather than simply shifting venues.

Beyond physical renewal, purpose-driven motivation requires emotional resilience and hope. Seasoned leaders expect cycles of breakthrough and breakdown, success and setback. They celebrate wins while avoiding complacency, grieving losses yet persevering with grit. Their conviction builds psychological strength to weather intense demands over long timeframes. With deep spiritual resources nurtured in community, meaningful work and private practices, motivation withstands tests that exhaust more superficial ambitions.

Choosing Positivity

Scientists have proven that sustained stress literally damages human physiology. With so much at stake in long-term quests, how can motivation outlast perpetual strain? The answer lies in choosing positivity amid pressure.

High achievers remain hopeful regarding eventual outcomes even while honestly assessing current difficulties. They celebrate incremental progress as markers of commitment paying off. Peers provide perspective when fatigue distorts effort-to-result ratios. Leaders avoid comparisons with those of different ages or advantages. Faith in larger purposes supersedes temporary measures.

This positivity refuses either naïve optimism or embittered pessimism. With discerning wisdom, motivation maintained over decades measures efforts through intentional lenses. Victories bring encouragement rather than arrogance, just as temporary defeats invoke perseverance rather than despair. Surrounded by support, conscious choice reframes stories we tell ourselves about the meaning of setbacks or delays.

By connecting today's tasks to clarified purposes envisioned for tomorrow, applying consistent discipline toward progress, renewing physical and emotional energy to serve long-term aims, and choosing positivity amid stress, motivation compounds daily for years until dreams become reality. With clear intention, focused investment, resilient hope and collective support, passionate persistence pays off in the end. Our world progresses through those relentless enough to keep believing, keep trying and keep taking the next step no matter what.

Prioritizing Holistic Health for Sustained Leadership

Effective leadership relies on resilience built through holistic wellbeing across mental, emotional, and physical realms. Neglecting health dimensions that fuel sustained performance can derail careers and organizational impact. The most successful leaders integrate self-care as non-negotiable, even amid extreme professional responsibilities.

Just as sharpened saws cut more cleanly than dull blades, leaders who regularly recharge can serve more responsively over lengthy tenures. Building margins between work and personal life provides mental distance from constant urgency as well as time to rejuvenate through interests beyond career ambitions. The most effective pacemakers establish rhythms of effort and recovery that reflect human needs rather than relentless machismo.

Leaders should feel comfortable setting boundaries around off-hours technology usage and guarding sacred family or hobby time. While higher purposes may inspire sacrifice during crunch periods, sustainable rhythms allow both organizations and households to flourish.

Prioritizing Holistic Health

In addition to life balance, well-rounded health requires nurturing physical, mental and social dimensions. Consistent exercise keeps stress hormones in check while stimulating energy and creativity. Good nutrition powers resilience to handle professional challenges as well as modeling workplace values. Protecting sleep facilitates cognitive clarity for high-stakes decisions rather than testimony to work martyrdom.

Seeking mental health support demonstrates courage, not weakness. Processing anxiety, grief or old traumas can lift heavy burdens carried silently for too long. Quality relationships provide empathetic sounding boards offering wisdom transcending individual perspectives. Even the most stoic leaders need receptivity and vulnerability to thrive.

Well-rounded self-care ultimately equips leaders to then invest in organizational and community wellness. Initiatives promoting flexible schedules, professional development, collaborative spaces, mental health coverage and healthy food options demonstrate that employee welfare drives sustainable excellence. What starts with personal priority reaches cultural fruition.

Leading by Long-Term Example

The cumulative pressures of senior authority require resilience reserves built up through self-awareness and holistic health habits over time. Leaders drained by sleep deprivation, chronic stress and narrow identity reach limits faster. Only the savvy remember fondly marathons completed rather than each exhausting mile.

By personally integrating self-care as non-negotiables now, rising leaders model sustainable expectations for those who will one day fill their shoes in turn. The hidden benefits will reveal themselves in crisis resilience, lifelong vocational passion and deeper family bonds long after daily strains fade. Transcendent legacies take shape slowly through daily wellbeing priorities that ultimately change cultures.

Succession Planning for Resilience

For leaders who have invested blood, sweat and tears into building organizations, considering one day departing elicits mixed emotions. Pride swells at accomplishments achieved through years of tireless effort. Yet anxiety bubbles up about sustaining that momentum for the future. This tends prods leaders toward working endless hours in hopes of cementing their legacy through sheer indispensable effort. However, the healthiest organizational cultures empower continuity by ensuring no single person's ongoing presence keeps the wheels turning. This process, known as succession planning, proves essential for founders and veteran executives alike to experience lasting personal fulfillment rather than chronic stress. Beyond benefiting company resilience, planning for eventual transitions secures a leader's sanity, satisfaction and significance for the long haul.

Escaping the Burden of Indispensability

Many rising stars find themselves promoted into leadership based on individual competency solving discrete problems. Their technical expertise or creative flair outshines peers, earning accolades and advancement. However, excelling as an individual contributor differs greatly from leading teams toward collaborative goals. Early success reinforces an unconscious belief one's solo efforts single-handedly determine organizational outcomes.

This high-stakes mindset breeds workaholism and anxiety no matter how skilled the leader. Subconsciously, they assume the company's welfare rests solely on their shoulders. Any cross-departmental friction or market turbulence incites personal overload around resolving every issue. Leaders operating from this assumption rarely disconnect or delegate. With hearts racing during brief sleepless nights, they conclude only their constant effort prevents catastrophic failure.

However, enlightened leaders eventually realize organizations only thrive through interconnected efforts far bigger than any solo contributor. Their flagship products rely on countless contributors working in alignment toward shared goals. By investing in others' development and constructing systems greater than themselves, wise leaders distribute creative authority and resilience.

This empowerment philosophy reaches its pinnacle in succession planning. When leaders intentionally groom others to someday fill their shoes, the weight of perceived world-holding lifts. Business continuity relies not on their personal ongoing tenure but on the culture and structures built to weather leadership transitions. Such leaders confidently prepare to pass the baton one day, at peace with their lasting influence outliving temporary roles.

Reaping the Reward of Patience

Despite understanding the logic of succession planning intellectually, following through requires emotional maturity. After pouring intense effort into building organizations from scratch, many leaders struggle handing over even partial control. They may hesitate promoting emerging leaders quickly. Instead, they unconsciously undermine rising talent in order to delay direct succession threats.

However, resistant hoarding authority for ego purposes risks stifling organizational growth. Younger team members bring fresh ideas, new capabilities and reaching demographics a stubborn leader may lack. Their raw potential both ensures relevance and brings deeper fulfillment by distributing leadership across generations. The young leaders whose careers blossom under patient guidance will later pay that investment forward in their own season of responsibility.

Therefore, embracing succession planning requires surrendering self-serving assumptions of perpetual control. But the rewards for doing so prove well worth temporary discomfort. Making room for others' contributions prompts innovation much faster than any solo efforts ever could. Leaders who demonstrate this level of secure self-awareness inspire incredible loyalty and performance from their teams. And they enjoy new capacity for long-term strategic vision no longer weighed down by daily execution strain. Stepping back from micromanagement presents bandwidth to guide cultural evolution.

Most meaningfully, when the long-awaited transition finally arrives, leaders who equipped eager successors through careful mentoring can depart confident the organization rests in trustworthy hands. This brings massive relief after years carrying exhaustive burdens alone. Right timing and thoughtful planning prevents leaving teams hanging; the new generation seamlessly carries forward momentum built collectively over the years. Releasing direct authority happens gracefully, with assurance one's lasting influence persists through those emerging leaders' growth.

Cultivating an Evergreen Legacy

Beyond immediate relief, succession planning also allows outgoing leaders' personal passions to continue benefiting the organization long-term. Through coaching and development conversations, they identify emerging innovators whose skills and interests match specific departments or initiatives still needing shaping. They deliberately groom next-generation specialists to elevate those domains for decades to come rather than narrowly perpetuate their own limitations.

Instead of insisting on rigid adherence to existing models, enlightened leaders facilitate experimentation with potential upgrades. They expect new leaders will redefine roles to better meet changing cultural needs. And they celebrate watching successors combine individual strengths with the organization's solid foundations toward something greater than imaginable alone. This evergreen view understands seasonality and disruption as essential for ongoing relevance and health.

Far beyond just resolving the logistical issue of empty positions, succession planning brings massive personal benefits to conscious leaders planning their eventual transitions. It allows them to release unrealistic messianic burdens through long-overdue delegation and distributed authority. It opens doors for fulfilling generational mentorship. And it secures future impact through continuity once direct tenure concludes. The leaders most fondly remembered decades later prove those self-assured enough to build cultures of resilient evolution that prosper beyond any singular prominent figurehead. Their legacy persists as new generations flourish through seeds early leaders planted for blossoming in due time. Succession planning allows outgoing veterans to experience gratitude for how far their teams have come rather than anxiety over letting go what identity they wrap up in continued responsibility. And that peace proves the ultimate reward for years of steadfast service any leader can pass on.

Key Takeaways & Final Thoughts on Building Resilience for the Long Haul

Key Takeaways:

- Clarifying core motivations and aligning daily tasks to overarching purpose sustains passion and drive over decades-long pursuits

- Balancing intense effort with restorative recovery prevents burnout that derails long-term goals

- Physical health factors like nutrition, exercise and sleep greatly impact mental resilience for handling leadership stresses

- Succession planning distributes responsibility across rising generations of talent, securing organizational continuity

- Implementing thoughtful transitions liberates veteran leaders to mentor successors without feeling indispensable or working endless hours

The Long Game: Practices for Sustaining Leaders over the Long Haul

Seasoned leaders often lament how they wish they knew earlier in their careers what experience has now taught them. The wisdom to pace oneself instead of constantly sprint, to build life margins that support demanding work, or to stay grounded in clarified purpose and values emerges only through difficult trials. However, by instilling key principles of sustainability early on, emerging leaders can build resilience to thrive over lengthy, fruitful careers rather than flame out seeking shortcut paths to success. Practices supporting physical health, whole-self development, generativity and wise succession planning all extend capacity to responsibly steward people, organizations and causes through seasons of change toward greater collective impact.

Cultivating resilience for the long haul first involves care for essential physical and emotional needs every leader shares despite different personalities or leadership styles. Paying attention to nutrition, movement, sleep and rest equips the body to handle unrelenting demands over decades without premature breakdown. Building life rhythms allowing sufficient recovery through interests outside of work keeps passion flowing by preventing vocational burnout. And protecting space for supportive community connections offers empathetic sounding boards when stressful decisions weigh heavily. Savvy leaders understand mental clarity essential for complex problem solving depends on caring well for emotional and physical realms in order to sustain peak performance when their teams most need them.

Looking beyond themselves, forward-focused leaders also pour effort into developing others for increased responsibility rather than eternally hoarding authority. They find deep fulfillment in seeing those they have coached go on to excel in areas matching their personal capabilities and passions. This succession mindset relinquishes illusion of full control but liberates leaders from feeling constantly indispensable to organizational success. By distributing ownership across empowered teams and ensuring continuity through transitions, they build resilience across groups instead of in isolation. Successors then replicate this cycle of raising up new waves of talent within their own spheres of influence. This rippling impact continues developing broad-based leadership for generations without reliance on lone heroic figures.

In closing, the world needs leaders who take seriously their calling to model healthy, ethical and sustainable practices while advancing collective wellbeing. But such journeys require resilience built thoughtfully over time, not grasping desperately for position. What priorities and accountability structures might help us lead wisely for the long haul?

Chapter Eight

Adaptability in Career Transitions

The concept of a career has undergone a dramatic evolution in recent decades. What was once a fixed pathway often spanning an entire working life has transformed into a dynamic, unpredictable journey requiring continuous growth and reinvention. As leaders and professionals, how do we steer our careers effectively amidst this uncertainty? By cultivating resilient mindsets and honing adaptable skillsets that empower us to stay relevant, create opportunity, and thrive through change.

Previously, career followed the noun structure – it was an entity secured with an employer that remained largely static over decades. You entered an organization in your youth, steadily progressed until retirement, received benefits for loyalty, and upheld dutiful reciprocity. However, continuous disruption has flipped this notion. Career is now better depicted as an action verb, demanding vigilance, versatility, and lifelong learning to sustain.

With verb-structured careers, while organizational commitment is still valued, it no longer guarantees continuity. Leaders today must operate with the mindset that at any time, through trends like restructuring, downsizing, offshoring, and automation, security can vanish. Does this sound intimidating? Shifting perspective illuminates the opportunities within the insecurity. Whereas noun-structured careers provided stability with little control, verb-structured careers offer immense agency to chart our trajectories amidst uncertainty.

Understanding Career Agility

What does career resilience and adaptability look like in action? The key is maintaining relevance by deliberately expanding our skills and connections to open new possibilities. Consider the following strategies:

Building a Track Record of Impact

Cultivating a compelling track record is about consistently exceeding expectations in impact and innovation. For instance, through identifying organizational challenges and spearheading solutions that advance key objectives beyond what a typical role entails. Not only does this expand capability and employability, but pushing past comfort zones also accelerates learning agility – a critical skill when operating in unpredictability.

Leaders should reflect on paramount priorities within their organizations and industries. What are glaring gaps, pain points, and growth opportunities? From this assessment, identify an initiative with the potential for breakthrough impact. Perhaps it entails piloting an experimental program to address customer friction points, constructing a people analytics framework to inform talent decisions, or leveraging emerging technologies like AI to advance R&D. The specific undertaking matters less than the willingness to spot voids and mobilize around solutions.

A track record rooted in value creation also showcases versatility critical for adaptability. When leaders can demonstrate the ability to identify needs and deliver results across diverse contexts, it inspires confidence in their capacity to do so regardless of circumstances. This versatility is what keeps talent resilient.

Cultivating Connections and Networks

Networks are the lifeblood of the verb-structured career, playing both an offensive and defensive role. On offense, robust professional networks unlock possibilities by channeling insider information about new initiatives and openings worthy of pursuit. They serve as referrers and champions to help secure roles aligned with our strengths and aspirations.

On defense, strong internal networks provide early signals when shifts like restructuring or downsizing gain momentum. With timeliness on our side, we can preemptively explore options, demonstrate value, and activate allies to influence more favorable outcomes. Externally, should severance occur, opportune connections stand at the ready to buoy our next endeavors.

Thus actively nurturing authentic, positive connections that span organizational silos and industries is profoundly beneficial. The most fertile networks come through consistently adding value – whether by making thoughtful introductions between parties with synergistic potential, providing mentoring and coaching to emerging talent, voicing informed perspectives that advance discourse, and more. When our modus operandi is generous service to others' potential, we organically develop safety nets and springboards.

Remaining Future-Fit in the Age of Automation

Lastly, as automation, AI, and other technologies transform how work gets done, future-proofing skills is non-negotiable. To stay ahead of workforce disruption, leaders should:

Continuously scan the horizon for game-changing innovations within their domain. Which technologies show early signs of breakthrough capability in areas we oversight? Where are competitors investing resources to harness automation and data analytics?

Probe and pressure-test current skills and knowledge against the trajectory of these work-altering tools. Will emerging algorithms and machines soon master abilities that historically distinguished our value? Prioritize closing these potential gaps.

Aggressively build out capabilities in machine-human collaboration, ethical oversight of technologies, data strategy, design thinking, and other future-oriented competencies melded with uniquely human strengths like creativity, empathy, and abstraction.

Commit to rapid prototyping and iteration rather than perfection – fail fast, learn faster. The shelf-life of skills is compressing. What suffices today will likely not suffice tomorrow.

While workplace volatility brings unease, redirecting our lens reveals liberating possibilities. As careers transform to verbs, we gain autonomy to steer our own course. By boldly strengthening networks, impact, and future-readiness, leaders can master career resilience and unlock new horizons of opportunity. The choice is ours – will we stand idle and beholden to change, or mobilize to direct it?

Cultivating Career Resilience Through Continuous Learning

Leaders must embrace continuous learning to sustain professional edge and marketability. But the learning required today extends beyond checking boxes on mandated training to stay compliant. True resilience demands proactively identifying seismic shifts within one's industry, assessing the competitor landscape, and discerning the breakthrough capabilities that will differentiate high performers tomorrow. It then requires mobilizing to close critical skill gaps before they emerge. Leaders who can rapidly retool their expertise to align with the future of work will maintain relevance despite external volatility.

This constant learning mindset understands career management as an iterative cycle, not a linear climb. There will likely be junctures along our leadership journey necessitating reskilling and reinvention to stay competitive. Rather than resist these inflection points, we can choose to embrace them as springboards to mastery of high-value skills.

Cultivating Transferable Skills Across Domains

Future-proof learning focuses less on domain expertise and more on cultivating versatile human capabilities that transcend specific technical needs. For instance, while machine learning may soon eclipse certain analytical tasks, innate human strengths like creativity, complex communication, and abstraction remain irreplaceable.

Leaders should take inventory of both technical and human skills they currently offer while assessing those likely to escalate in importance within their industry and role. Are there opportunities to further develop strengths like design thinking for human-centric solutions, data literacy, ethical risk evaluation, cross-domain systems analysis, and other future-oriented capabilities? Can some specialized expertise be repositioned to higher value in adjacent spaces?

Beyond expanding individual skills, consider how entire roles may evolve. Could demonstrable experience spearheading automation technology, overseeing AI integration, or leading digitally-powered teams become vital in setting leaders apart? By spotting the vectors of change early and deliberately gaining Exposure through short-term projects, job rotations, or temporary assignments, leaders amplify adaptability.

Convert Learning Into Opportunity

Continuous learning is most effective when parlayed directly into new ventures that expand scope. For instance, after sharpening data and analytics acumen, one might identify an untapped business challenge where these skills could drive transformation. Perhaps legacy practices currently rely on intuitive decisions versus evidence-based insights. Demonstrating capacity to build analytics dashboards, run controlled pilot studies, and translate findings into high-impact programs showcases versatility.

This undertaking both applies emerging skills and strengthens visibility and credibility in that domain. Other examples might include volunteering to lead a cross-functional automation initiative, revamping customer experience through human-centered design principles, or optimizing internal operations through process excellence methodologies.

Leaders should reflect on priority areas for innovation within their organizations and target opportunities to spearhead solutions that leverage their expanding skillsets. Even small-scale experiments harness continuous learning to heighten resilience.

The Case for Career Reinvention

While proactive reskilling centers on getting ahead of change, times may arise when more reactive pivots become necessary. Industry disruption, restructuring, or technical leaps can radically reshape a role, rendering once-prized expertise less relevant. When facing such inflection points, leaders able to rapidly reskill and even reinvent themselves in alignment with emerging needs builds resilience.

Technical skills now have an ever-decreasing half-life. But when anchored in timeless human strengths like curiosity, empathy, creativity, and determination, leaders can fluidly retool. To ease difficult transitions, focus first on transferable capabilities from past roles, recognizing human skills remain constant even if technical needs shift. This mindset builds confidence to assimilate new competencies faster. Maintain networks who can endorse and advise to accelerate gaining traction in a new space.

While many resist starting over, the clean slate of reinvention brings opportunity to redirect our careers toward genuine passions and making meaningful impact. With an openness to explore emerging domains and dedication to rapid skill-building, leaders can unlock pathways to drive change through work truly aligned with personal and organizational purpose.

Continuous learning is no longer optional - it is the price of entry to sustain career resilience. But when undertaken with strategy and imagination, it becomes the competitive edge that unlocks a wealth of possibility. Let uncertainty give way to agency. Transform disruption into opportunity. Chart your leadership course with skillsets primed for the future.

Adapting to Industry Shifts with Adaptive Leadership

Disruption has become the norm across most industries, fueled by forces like emerging technologies, changing consumer behaviors, globalization, and more. For leaders, navigating these tumultuous waters requires mastering the art of adaptability. We can no longer cling to static leadership styles rooted in past success - yesterday's approaches lack resilience for uncertain futures. Thriving now demands accurately assessing shifting contexts, flexing our approach accordingly, and continuously honing the capability to adjust course amid volatility.

Cultivating an Adaptive Mindset

The foundation of adaptive leadership begins with mindset - embracing fluidity over rigidity in how we operate, lead teams, drive change, and even view ourselves as leaders. Given the speed of change today, there is no permanent destination. Rather than resisting this reality or struggling against forces outside our control, we can choose to become connoisseurs of change.

This starts by scrutinizing our reflexive assumptions of what constitutes effective leadership. Do statements like "a good leader must exude absolute confidence and decisive vision" or "vulnerability betrays weakness" still serve us? Do they allow space for critical thinking, collective wisdom, and course-correcting? Sweeping away outdated mental models clears room for more dynamic frameworks better suited for uncertainty.

With more open minds, we can sharpen awareness of the interdependent forces driving industry shifts - from emerging consumer expectations and behaviors to potential technology disruption. We can track competitive moves while scanning parallel sector pivots for instructive patterns. This immerses us within the realities redefining our landscape so we lead grounded in strategic clarity, not isolation. Armed with insights into change drivers, we can then evaluate their implications on vision, structure, talent needs and culture to chart responsive strategies. Our teams require this decisiveness and direction setting even amidst ambiguity.

Assessing and Applying Leadership Styles

Transparency around change enables aligning leadership approaches to evolving demands. For instance, seasons requiring bold vision or transformation may call for more charismatic, inventive leadership to mobilize and inspire teams towards radical solutions. However, realizing ambitious ideas demands analytical discipline, structured execution and accountability - well-suited to a more directive, operational style.

Here we see adaptive leadership's fluidity in action - the ability to pivot styles situationally based on contextual needs and personal strengths without clinging to one approach. Perhaps divisions of the organization need different leadership given contrasting change impacts and maturity levels. Teams craving upskilling may warrant more relationships-focused, connective leadership. While overwhelmed groups might respond better to authoritative decision-making to reduce uncertainty. The goal is attuning leadership dial to each context.

We can evaluate our adaptability through various assessment frameworks - examining communication patterns, problem solving tactics, feedback mechanisms and change orientation. Role playing complex scenarios, peer exchanges and even personality tests also reveal blindspots. Transparent feedback loops ensure teams feel empowered to challenge assumptions and suggest alternative paths if rigid leadership grows misaligned with emerging realities. Rather than resist criticism, adaptive leaders invite debate and leverage collective ingenuity to pressure-test decisions amid disruption.

The Role of Allies and Mentors

Finally, investing in allies and mentors accelerates learning. Leadership coaches trained in navigating uncertainty provide sounding boards to process complex change. Peer networks across industries share learnings around modern challenges from digital transformation to ethics oversight. Multi-generational mentors check assumptions we overlook. And reverse mentors like early career talent offer frontline insights on shifting workforce expectations.

This landscape of diverse support keeps leaders attuned to changes immediately affecting customers and markets as well as those creeping over horizons. It also lends empathy, reassurance and perspective when disruptive forces necessitate exhausting reinvention. Through whatever industry storms arise, the adaptive leader realizes the power of community. Transformation becomes a shared journey of aligned leaders progressing into the future, stronger with every bend.

Establishing Thought Leadership

While often associated with specific disciplines like technology, business, or politics, thought leadership transcends any single domain. It is defined by the ability to zoom out and identify unseen patterns, make unconventional connections and discern how seismic shifts may unfold. Thought leadership probes unexplored frontiers of understanding to reveal opportunity. It also brings People together around emergent ideas and progressive solutions not bound by convention.

This ethos of inquiry and advancement is precisely why cultivating thought leadership and online influence is so vital today. More interconnected than ever before, society's most complex challenges resist siloed answers. Real impact demands new frameworks, unlikely alliances and inspired multidisciplinary action. There has likely never been a time riper for bold thought leadership rooted in ethics and the collective good. The question becomes - how can we realize this potential?

The Platform for Catalyzing Conversations

With billions of users worldwide, social networks offer unprecedented reach. But crafting posts in isolation earns little influence. Thought leadership is sparked through conversation - listening intently as patterns emerge and synergies surface across diverse voices. Social platforms allow catalyzing these rich dialogues.

This starts by creating content - written, visual or audio - that provides novel analysis of known challenges. For example, a leader renowned for non-profit management might post a commentary examining links between philanthropy and the rise of billionaire space exploration. Such interdisciplinary connections illuminate less obvious dimensions ripe for discourse. We can also spotlight emerging leaders and models that signal more promising futures across domains like education, medicine or responsible technology. Content centered on understanding and advancement tends to attract kindred minds eager for progress.

Yet even paradigm-shifting ideas hold little weight without credibility rooted in expertise and experience. This is why regularly publishing value-adding perspectives clarifies our distinct viewpoint. Over time, the novelty of our angles and solutions earns distinction as audience and influence grow.

Cultivating Community Through Engagement

While strong content provides the fodder for dialogue, active engagement brings it to life. Thought leadership requires exchanging ideas, debating divergent views and co-creating towards shared goals. Are there peers or emerging voices posting intriguing related content? Can we thoughtfully highlight alternative perspectives to advance discourse? Comments and positive highlights signal others the value in joining larger discussions.

We might also respond directly to audience questions and feedback to strengthen ties. Or share community content with our networks when it aligns to collective interests. Facilitating rich peer exchanges forges bonds while clarifying our own positions. It also seeds future collaborations to synthesize insights across groups.

Partnerships to Amplify Impact

The most resonant thought leaders understand progress demands allyship. Once established as a credible voice, we can magnify reach and impact through strategic partnerships. Such collaborations also benefit peers and partners.

For example, contributing unique commentary pieces for a partner's blog or podcast expands visibility within aligned networks eager for our viewpoints. We might also cohost discussion panels, interactive webinars or conference workshops combining distinct expertise. Joint research projects, white papers and multimedia series allow conveying synergistic insights in compelling formats. Powerful affiliations elevate partners' credibility while allowing us to lead vital conversations with broader audiences. The key lies in partnerships rooted in shared values and vision, not promotional exchanges. Through purpose-driven allyship, we compound awareness and inspiration beyond our bubbles.

While becoming recognized thought leaders requires diligence, leaders already command extensive knowledge otherwise untapped. Social channels offer conduits to synthesize our perspectives collectively around the change we wish to see.

Key Takeaways & Final Thoughts on Adaptability in Career Transitions

Key Takeaways:

- Career trajectories are increasingly unpredictable, requiring continuous adaptation and growth mindsets focused on building transferable skills rather than fixed expertise. Leaders must proactively expand capabilities and networks to open new possibilities amid volatility.

- With careers transforming into iterative journeys, leaders should view inflection points as opportunities for reinvention aligned to emerging needs and personal purpose, rather than reacting with rigidity. Mindsets anchored in curiosity, determination and lifelong learning ease difficult transitions.

- Continuous learning is now non-negotiable to remain competitive and employable. Leaders should identify seismic shifts within their industry and take inventory of human strengths versus technical skills requiring augmentation. Committing to rapid prototyping and skilling application keeps expertise relevant.

- Establishing a track record of impact that exceeds expectations provides resilience by showcasing versatility and capacity to create value amid changing contexts. Leaders should identify organizational needs prime for innovative solutions that allow exercising emerging capabilities.

- Relationships and networks serve as springboards to buoy leaders through transitions. Intentionally nurturing connections, allyship and mutual value exchange facilitates access to opportunities, insights and influence.

Sustainable Success in the New Era of Careers

The modern world of work grows increasingly dynamic amid continuous technological, social and political disruption. As automation, AI and economic turbulence redefine jobs and skills, the days of linear career progression within stable institutions expire. Navigating this landscape requires resilience and adaptability unlike any before.

The leaders who will thrive are those embracing careers as open-ended journeys of reinvention and impact unconfined by convention. They actively cultivate versatility, knowledge and connections to capitalize on emerging opportunities. They view volatility as the force that unlocks possibilities and catalyzes growth rather than an obstacle to enduring success.

While disruption may cost fleeting moments of stability, the autonomy, agency and lifelong learning it galvanizes allows achieving career goals profoundly aligned with evolving marketplace needs and personal purpose. No longer beholden to prescriptive paths, we craft our own.

Leadership today demands flexibility and foresight. But anchoring our direction in empathy, human strengths and determination equips us to fluidly retool along the way. With these as our compass, we can chart courses to drive change through whatever unseen frontiers or unprecedented challenges ahead.

Are you ready to lead amid the winds of change? What possibilities will you unleash? The only constant we know is perpetual disruption. Shall we master its channels and redirect towards progress?

Chapter Nine

The Path Towards Ethical Leadership

Leadership plays a pivotal role in shaping organizational culture and employee experiences. When leaders uphold strong ethical values and standards, it fosters an environment of trust, respect, and transparency. However, leaders also have an enormous capacity to damage morale, performance, and the bottom line when they exercise authority without integrity. As society continues to scrutinize businesses and call for more conscientious practices, developing ethical leadership strategies has become a pressing need to guide companies into the future.

What defines an ethical leader? Ethical leaders display behaviors such as honesty, care for people, justice and fairness, responsible management, and commitment to community. Through their words and actions, they communicate clear expectations for ethical conduct organization-wide. Research shows that ethical leadership correlates strongly with higher employee engagement, satisfaction, creativity, and performance. It also mitigates many pressing issues facing today's corporations, like discrimination, harassment, fraud, and poor transparency. Employees feel valued under leaders who treat them with dignity and respect. When people see leaders adhering to a moral code, they gain trust in the system and feel empowered to speak up about misconduct without fear of retaliation.

Ultimately, ethical leaders enhance public perception and help attract and retain top talent.

Cultivating ethical leadership requires concerted, ongoing effort at all levels of an organization. It starts with those at the very top setting the tone for the values and behaviors that shape culture. Leaders must clearly define ethics policies and procedures while also serving as role models through their day-to-day actions. This includes transparent communication, admitting mistakes, listening to input across the organizational hierarchy, and rewarding integrity. Ongoing ethics training programs ensure everyone understands expectations and can recognize potential issues. Establishing safe, anonymous reporting procedures gives employees an outlet to voice concerns without fear of consequences. Regular audits help identify problem areas early before they spiral out of control. Addressing infractions swiftly, justly, and with appropriate consequences for all involved serves as a deterrent for future wrongdoing. When unethical incidents do occur, ethical leaders analyze the context without blaming individuals and implement controls to prevent recurrences.

While cultivating ethical leadership takes concerted planning and effort, the rewards make it more than worthwhile. Companies with reputations for ethical practices enjoy higher esteem in their industries and local communities. Employees feel satisfied and motivated when treated as valuable contributors rather than commodities. Customers develop greater brand loyalty when they trust in an organization's transparency and intentions. Over time, the compounding benefits of ethical leadership—from innovation to productivity to profitability—build substantial momentum to carry companies successfully through global market volatility. Wise investments in people and culture repay exponentially when crises hit.

Of course, leaders face tremendous pressure to deliver short term results which often competes with ideals of ethical leadership. Navigating these realities while upholding ethical standards represents one of the greatest challenges for modern organizational leaders. It requires courage, foresight, and commitment to stay the course even when tempted by quick fixes or workarounds that violate values and integrity. Leaders must recognize that lasting success depends on building robust ethical foundations rather than chasing immediate gains at any cost. With constant vigilance, patience, and care for human needs, today's leaders can model the way towards a more ethical future where organizations thrive sustainably.

Understanding Ethical Leadership

Ethical leadership centers on conducting business with integrity. Unlike authoritarian styles focused strictly on profits, ethical leaders demonstrate moral courage inside and outside the office. Their actions align with ethical principles of honesty, fairness, responsibility, and care for people and society. Ethical leaders uplift standards by confronting misconduct even when inconvenient. They model high expectations through accountability, transparency, admitting mistakes, and rewarding integrity. Employees gain trust and feel empowered to speak up about ethics concerns without fear of retaliation.

Challenges and Criticism

In today's volatile, complex business climate, leaders face intense pressures that challenge ethical leadership. Short term goals often conflict with principles. Critics contend idealistic ethical standards hinder profitability or competitive edge. Indeed, many recent corporate scandals and political transgressions illustrate a crisis of leadership integrity across sectors. However, ethical shortcuts usually incur higher long term costs than benefits. Building robust ethical foundations better positions organizations to thrive sustainably amid market uncertainty.

Implementing Ethical Practices

While upholding ethical leadership presents difficulties, the rewards warrant commitment to the challenge. Concrete policies and procedures codify expected conduct. Ongoing training ensures organizational alignment behind ethical standards. Anonymous reporting channels give employees an outlet for addressing concerns early before they escalate. Swift, fair, and consistent accountability for infractions deters future misconduct. Regular audits identify problem areas needing improvement. However, rules only work when leaders model desired behaviors daily. Achieving an ethical culture requires patience, courage, and care for human needs through turbulent times.

The Bottom Line

When rooted in sound ethics, leadership builds employee trust, satisfaction, engagement, creativity, and performance essential for long term success. A culture of integrity and care for people also translates into stronger external reputation, community goodwill, and customer loyalty - competitive advantages no shortcut can replicate. While cultivating ethical leadership demands vigilance, the dividends over time empower sustainable, responsible growth.

The importance of ethical leadership

Leadership plays a pivotal role in shaping organizational culture, guiding strategy, and influencing stakeholders. Therefore, leaders carry an enormous capacity to uplift or damage a company's reputation, performance, and bottom line depending on how ethically they wield authority. In today's complex global economy filled with volatility and uncertainty, organizations need resilient leaders who can make difficult decisions with integrity when facing rising scrutiny. Companies that prioritize ethical leadership reap tangible rewards like improved recruitment, innovation, productivity, profitability, and long-term sustainability.

What Constitutes an Ethical Leader?

Ethical leaders display behaviors aligned with moral values like honesty, integrity, fairness, responsibility, and caring for people, communities, and social justice. They communicate clear expectations and accountability at all levels while serving as role models for desired conduct. This encompasses admitting mistakes, listening to input from across the organizational hierarchy, rewarding integrity, and confronting wrongdoing transparently even when inconvenient. Employees gain trust in leaders who treat them with dignity, empathy, and respect. Ethical leaders enhance morale, engagement, and performance by inspiring shared purpose and giving people autonomy to carry out tasks responsibly. Their example empowers others to have courageous conversations that reinforce ethical norms.

Overcoming Criticism and Challenges

Cultivating ethical leadership requires concerted, ongoing diligence across all organizational operations. Leaders must clearly define ethics policies and procedures while also walking the talk in their everyday actions. This ethical foundation provides a compass to guide decisions and behavior when facing intense pressure to compromise standards. Critics argue adhering to seemingly lofty ethical ideals lowers competitiveness or hinders profitability compared to more authoritarian command-and-control leadership methods. However, research shows organizations gain more over time from ethical integrity than short-term gains from dubious shortcuts. Ethical cultures experience less misconduct, fraud, turnover, and reputational damage. They attract top talent who thrive through positive empowerment rather than fear or pressure. While establishing ethical leadership poses challenges, the rewards warrant whatever efforts necessary to achieve it.

Strategies for Building an Ethical Culture

While lofty aspirations provide vision, leaders must operationalize ethics through concrete policies and procedures. Individuals wishing to champion ethical culture from any position can:

- Lead by example in your own conduct first. Model integrity, accountability, and courage to admit mistakes. Seek feedback and self-reflect honestly. Your personal credibility enables influencing others.

- Advocate for explicit ethics codes and standards aligned with company values. Help shape and regularly review policies as contexts evolve over time. Codified guidelines clarify expectations.

- Spearhead ongoing training programs explaining the importance behind ethics rules. Ensure everyone understands rationale driving proper conduct beyond blind rule compliance. Update trainings to address real cases and emerging risks.

- Design safe spaces for people to discuss concerns without fear of retaliation. Anonymized reporting channels like suggestion boxes or confidential hotlines encourage addressing issues early before they compound.

- Promote transparency expectations across communications. Discreetly tackle ethics concerns raised respectfully through two-way dialogue. Develop escalation procedures for handling repeated or egregious misconduct judiciously.

- Keep ethics conversations ongoing to reinforce norms collectively. Facilitate workshops or community forums for people to share perspectives, dilemmas, and insights anonymously without judgement.

- Spotlight positive examples of integrity. Recognize those who personify desired behaviors through rewards or internal communications. But avoid perceived favoritism by upholding consistent accountability.

- Analyze infractions thoroughly once exposed to understand their genesis rather than jumping to discipline without context. Seek root causes and thoughtful remedies tailored to different personnel levels involved.

- Welcome independent internal and external audits non-defensively to highlight areas for ethical culture improvement. Develop controls targeting frequent issue triggers early before problems multiply.

- Keep iterating ethics strategies as contexts evolve over time. Apply lessons learned to strengthen vulnerable spaces proactively. Continual collective vigilance prevents complacency around ethical culture.

The path towards integrity requires patience, care, and moral courage in the face of adversity. But organizational cultures cultivated by ethical leadership compound returns over time through enhanced trust, engagement, retention, and performance. Lead from the front with your actions, or support quietly from behind the scenes through patience and understanding. Progress ultimately depends on each person's commitment to ethics, empathy, and respect at all levels.

The Ripple Effects of Ethical Leadership

Research shows companies perceived as ethical enjoy higher esteem among customers, communities, and industries. Stakeholders develop greater trust in transparent communication and intentions from ethical leaders. Public relations crises get resolved faster when organizations have credibility rooted in integrity. A culture deliberately shaped by ethical leadership motivates employees through inspiration rather than pressure tactics. Satisfied workers remain loyal to companies that treat them with respect and care. Turnover declines substantially when people feel heard and valued for their contributions. High retention preserves critical institutional knowledge. Talented candidates gravitate towards ethical employers offering healthy work-life balance and development opportunities. Companies avoiding scandals and lawsuits reduce costs associated with misconduct dramatically over years. Global brands cultivating ethical practices across international offices and supply chains gain advantages adapting to different cultural norms. While ethical leadership requires committing to responsible growth, the compounding returns over time empower organizations to sustain success.

Modeling the Way Forward

Ulimately, leadership faces constant tension balancing idealism and reality. The future depends on businesses proving capitalism with compassion reigns superior to outdated notions of profits over people. This precipitates upon today's leaders courageously modeling ethical integrity despite temptations to compromise. Maintaining high standards through volatile times requires commitment to humanistic visions beyond quarterly earnings. Leadership is not a title - it is a mindset backed by moral conviction. Ethical leaders acknowledge business cannot thrive functioning detached from societal context or human needs. They understand lasting positive change cascades from fair and responsible conduct, not authoritarian demands. Renewed focus on ethics and empathy in leadership training programs promises to shape a new generation guided by conscience, not just credentials. Indeed, anyone at any level can pivot their leadership approach towards mentoring through inspiration rather than wielding power through fear.

The Consequences of Compromised Ethics

Amid high-profile scandals and corruption, the business sector grapples with perceptions of prioritizing profits over ethical conduct. However, organizations permeability to moral compromises risks tangible operational, financial and reputational damage. Mitigating misconduct requires establishing integrity as a core competency embedded throughout policies, procedures, and culture. Ethical foundations enable sound, sustainable success.

Legal Consequences of Unethical Practices

Flouting regulations often extracts harsh legal penalties, including lawsuits, criminal charges, and heavy fines erasing short-term gain. Executives violating fiduciary duties or enabling harmful internal climates face steep personal liability risks jail time. While no regulations fully inoculate against determined unethical behavior, non-compliance fundamentally jeopardizes organizational interests and social license to operate. Even occasional legal breaches signal deficient integrity standards require urgent strengthening.

Impacts on Employee Performance & Relations

Toxic cultures bred by ethical relativism damage productivity and morale. Staff become disengaged when incentives seem to reward dishonest scheming rather than merit. Mistrust proliferates when ethical voids at the top signal acceptable conduct lines remain unclear. Anxiety around possible cheating brews resentment even among rule-abiders navigating office politics. Leader credibility nosedives absent accountability for double standards. Suppressed development potential from corrupted, demoralized teams harvests steep opportunity costs over time.

Reputational Ruin and Lost Trust

Flagrant scandals or chronic misconduct erosion broadcast widely in today's hyper-connected landscape collect lasting public contempt towards culpable institutions. Internet outrage endures permanently even after window-dressing image rehabilitation efforts. Investor confidence plummets around perceived unethical organizations, increasing capital costs. Talented candidates shy from tarnished employers. Long-loyal customers abandon brands associating too closely with value-conflicted controversies. Though contextual nuances exist in ethical grey zones, reputational stains of lost integrity prove extremely difficult to scrub.

Core Principles for Organizational Integrity

At its core, ethical leadership embodies conducting business with integrity and care for people. Unlike authoritarian styles, ethical leaders uphold moral values like honesty, fairness, equality, accountability, respect, and trustworthiness. These principles provide a moral compass for navigating complex decisions. Ethical leaders confront misconduct and wrongdoing with courage, even when inconvenient. Their actions signal standards for integrity at all levels. Employees gain inspiration to advance ethical best practices when they see leaders walking the talk.

Key Ethical Leadership Principles

Several central principles characterize an ethical leadership approach:

- *Fairness* requires defining clear expectations and applying consistent accountability without favoritism when addressing poor decisions or misconduct. No one receives special treatment outside the systematic application of rules.

- *Accountability* means leaders take ownership of mistakes without blaming external factors. Willingly admitting errors and shortcomings demonstrates courage and transparency vital for trust.

- *Trust* flourishes when leaders follow through consistently on promises and commitments. Honesty and trust fuel open communication to tackle difficult issues constructively.

- *Equality* emphasizes dignity and common humanity. Ethical leaders value all voices and contributions while rejecting discrimination harmful to human potential.

- *Respect* embodies considering different viewpoints, experiences, and needs to inform inclusive decisions. Leaders demonstrate empathy and care for people as holistic human beings rather than just employees.

Challenges in Application

These principles provide guideposts for ethical leadership, but real-world application poses challenges. Fairness perceptions depend heavily on context and interpretation. Blind rule compliance backfires without understanding situational factors, individual differences, and unintended consequences. Quick accountability reactions could overlook root causes requiring patience to unravel. Trust building requires maintaining confidences and transparency carefully to avoid counterproductive breaches. Truth-telling risks conflict without thoughtful framing and mediation skills. Equality ideals must reconcile with merit-based rewards vital for motivation. Respectful discourse needs structured facilitation when emotions escalate out of control. Despite complications, concrete policies, procedures, modelling from the top, and open dialogue forums aid ethical culture embedding.

Shared Responsibility at All Levels

Cultivating ethical leadership ultimately requires daily effort and shared responsibility at all levels. It starts with boards and executives codifying ethical principles within formal policies. But verbose rulebooks mean little without accompanying actions demonstrating desired conduct consistently. Middle managers face accountability for translating ethical aspirations into everyday team practices. Supervisors play a pivotal role modelling caring, respect, and integrity during individual interactions. However, frontline employees equally share duty to uphold ethical standards personally while encouraging peers towards positive expression of ethics. Across hierarchies, maintaining ethical culture relies on collective vigilance in upholding principles, speaking out against misconduct, participating in ethics conversations, and showing grace around inadvertent missteps.

A Framework for Principled Decision-Making

Ethical integrity provides the load-bearing pillars upon which sustainable success gets built. Values shape assumptions driving behaviors which accumulate into culture. Leaders seeking enduring excellence recognize ethical foundations as essential organizational infrastructure deserving thoughtful construction using time-tested materials. Just as strong buildings weather storms through resilient flexible designs, companies cultivated upon moral bedrock navigate change guided by an inner compass aligned to true North principles.

Ethics formal codification within policy declarations signifies intent without guaranteeing implementation. Pretty platitudes made public mean little if not actively operationalized daily through decisions at all levels. Leaders own responsibility for translating aspirational words into aligned actions. However, the ethical task requires shared vigilance across hierarchies to uphold, improve and repair integrity infrastructure constantly. Building ethical organizations for the long-term demands incorporating moral perspectives into deliberative processes long before crises force reactionary repairs.

Defining Ethical Values and Obligations

Fundamental ethical values like integrity, responsibility, respect, fairness and compassion provide an intuitive starting point. But moving from conceptual abstraction to practical application in ambiguous contexts remains challenging terrain. Navigating complex dilemmas and conflicts of interest where ethical principles seemingly collide rather than converge requires insight into root motivations and character. Yet organizations cannot offload the entirety of ethical burdens onto individuals alone. Institutions bear duties of care and justice beyond narrow self-interest. Ethical business balances profit-seeking through open markets with concern for societal and environmental sustainability. Legal compliance establishes minimum baselines for ethical conduct but fails to reach aspirational moral peaks organizations should strive towards in honoring highest humanistic values.

Cultivating Shared Understanding Around Values

Leaders play instrumental roles in cultivating shared ethical understanding. They must spark ongoing conversations to challenge assumptions, raise awareness of blind spots, unpack context behind apparent conflicts and locate integration opportunities. Every team member deserves chances to voice moral perspectives respected as valid interpretations of collectively held principles rather than problematic disruptions to efficiency. Leaders modeling humility create psychologically safe spaces for morally mature dialogue to take place multidirectionally across hierarchies. Through supportive exchange, clarity gets reached on ethical applications tailored appropriately to circumstances and characters involved. Over time, the corresponding enrichment of relationships builds resilient capacities to navigate values tensions constructively together.

Commitments to Consistency and Self-Reflection

However, talk means little without walking the walk consistently to back up espoused ethical ideals. Hypocrisy and double standards destroy integrity faster than anything. Leaders above all face responsibilities to self-reflect deeply on how their actions either strengthen or erode the ethical foundations they publicly champion. They must question whether incentives and Key Performance Indicators overemphasize superficial metrics compared to deeper humanistic developmental progress. Consistently aligning internal organizational systems and processes to reflect stated values requires analyzing how everyday choices cumulatively shape cultural realities over years through intended and unintended consequences. Leaders modelling ethical accountability stand ready to receiving feedback from all levels and adjust course promptly when misalignments get exposed between principles and practices.

Constructing Safeguards Against Ethical Erosions

Given ever-present realities of ethical erosion, organizations must engineer control systems to monitor and manage threats proactively. Focused risk assessment spotlights vulnerabilities related to financial controls, harassment, discrimination, health and safety, conflicts of interest, privacy, and environmental issues warranting priority mitigation. Tailored policies codify expected conduct aligned to values. Anonymous reporting channels empower safe escalation of suspected breaches. Swift, fair investigatory procedures balance rights of confidentiality for accusers and accused with impartial examination of circumstances to determine reasonable responsive actions. Independent auditing bodies provide external objective performance assessments to prevent insular conformity bias and prompt self-correction. Comprehensive ethics training immerses employees within dilemmas illustrating how values apply differently across contexts to build sound moral judgement capabilities. Engineering multilayered integrity infrastructure promises resilience amidst turbulence.

Modelling Morals in Action

Yet technical controls and rule-based compliance ultimately fail without leadership modelling ethical behavior daily through low-key, high-visibility actions. Studies demonstrate equitable conduct and compassion displayed towards employees get mirrored externally to customers and community. Leaders uplifting inner dignity for marginalized voices plant seeds growing eventually into social justice movements transforming societies for the better. But the inverse equally holds true. Toxic self-serving cultures shaped by ruthless executives damage integrity foundations in ways no subsequent leader can easily rebuild without substantial demolition and reconstruction efforts first. Ethical leaders thus understand the gravity of responsibility entrusted to them as guardians charting direction amidst crosscurrents. They guide with moral courage pointing True North.

Promoting Openness, Inclusion and Principled Dissent

Key to sustaining ethical health remains maintaining openness to constructive dissent grounded in shared principles. Leaders promote psychological safety for respectful debate and discussion regarding ethics policies, practices and decisions. They understand healthy cultures embrace dissonance as catalysts for innovation rather than threats to conformity. Seeking diverse inputs and whistleblower concerns before destructive escalations signals organizational maturity and trust to handle discord. However, leaders balance transparency with sober acknowledgement of reasonable confidentiality requirements involving personnel matters, health details, pending legal issues and proprietary intellectual property. Through modelling integrity and compassion in addressing tensions as they emerge, leaders reinforce moral social norms cooperatively with employees as ethics co-champions.

The path towards integrity remains long with humbling setbacks assured along the way. However, organizations diligently cultivating ethical decision-making based upon moral convictions discover the means to tap human potentials beyond what rules and incentives can extract through carrots and sticks alone. By aiming higher to realize values honoring human dignity, they harvest multiplied returns benefiting all stakeholders in due course.

Key Takeaways & Final Thoughts on The Path Towards Ethical Leadership

Key Takeaways:

- Ethical foundations provide the load-bearing pillars for constructing sustainable success amid volatility. Values shape assumptions driving behaviors accumulating into culture over years.

- Leaders own responsibility for translating aspirational words into aligned ethical actions. However, cultivating integrity requires shared vigilance across hierarchies to uphold standards daily.

- Navigating complex dilemmas requires insight into root motivations and character. Legal compliance provides ethical baselines, but organizations should aspire towards moral peaks honoring humanistic values.

- Fostering ethical understanding involves ongoing multidirectional dialogues challenging assumptions and locating integration opportunities when principles seemingly conflict.

- Hypocrisy and double standards erode integrity rapidly. Leaders must self-reflect on how actions and incentives strengthen or undermine publicly championed values.

- Controls and compliance ultimately fail without leaders modelling ethical behavior daily through low-key, high visibility caring actions that get mirrored externally.

Sustaining Ethical Momentum Across Generations

The extensive dialogue explored the intricate complexities involved in cultivating ethical integrity within modern organizations. While lofty aspirations provide initial vision, translating values into consistent daily actions requires vigilant collective effort. However, the rewards of moral conviction tap human potentials beyond what rules and carrots alone can extract through compliance.

Leaders play pivotal roles modelling and championing ethics through visibility caring acts and compassionate response to dissent. Their example shapes assumptions driving behaviors accumulating into culture — for good or ill. Ethical foundations, carefully constructed, provide load-bearing pillars supporting sustainable success amid volatility.

Yet thriving through turbulence depends on sustaining ethical momentum across generations. Tomorrow's leaders must internalize the wisdom around uphill challenges, but also hear calls to courage. Upon strong shared foundations, they must build even better through creativity and care. And by aiming higher to realize values honoring human dignity, they stand to harvest multiplied returns benefiting all. Where vitue guides, progress follows.

The path towards integrity remains long, with humbling setbacks assured. However, a forward-looking question presents itself - if not now, when? And if not through today's leaders, then through whom? The ethical organizational journey begins by single step. But destiny gets determined by the direction chosen.

Chapter Ten

Crisis Management for Leaders

Crises inevitably transpire in today's turbulent business landscape, often without warning. Yet research reveals a staggering 60-70% of executives feel unprepared to lead through turbulent times. Why this gap, and how can leaders equip themselves to respond effectively when chaos strikes? The answers involve intentionally developing crisis resilience.

Envision two senior executives impacting by an sudden scandal threatening brand reputation. Executive A freezes, overwhelmed by the onslaught of scrutiny as events spiral rapidly outside their control. Executive B responds swiftly, having invested in understanding potential risks and constructing robust response frameworks. They activate crisis protocols, coordinate stakeholders, get ahead of the narrative, and mitigate damage through decisive leadership.

The divergence traces back to the leaders' mindsets before storms gathered on the horizon. Executive A never envisioned themselves at the helm of a crisis, lacking critical competencies when flooded with complexity. Executive B accepted turmoil as inevitable, intentionally preparing through proactive learning. When volatility struck, Executive B remained ready to respond strategically. Their resilient thinking served as the first line of defense.

Cultivating a Crisis-Ready Mindset

A crisis-ready leader understands unpredictable events will arise and readies themselves mentally long before chaos erupts. This involves regularly scanning the horizon for gathering storms other executives may dismiss or downplay. It means running fire drills to stress test organizational resilience, peppering teams with "what if" scenarios that imagine untested vulnerabilities. Such perspective prepares leaders cognitively and emotionally to respond intentionally rather than reactively when faced with high stakes dilemmas offering narrow windows for response.

Resilient leaders further accept crises as professional development opportunities disguised as threats, not viewing them fatalistically as threats to be avoided. By examining case studies detailing how other executives navigated turbulent contexts, leaders can extract lessons to shape their own crisis management philosophy while identifying personal areas for growth. Such leaders appreciate that crisis response requires different competencies than traditional leadership, intentionally targeting these skills for mentorship.

Constructing A Response Framework

With an empowered crisis-ready mindset, leaders can then construct comprehensive crisis management frameworks customized to their organizational risks. This advanced preparation separates those who simply react in the heat of catastrophe from those prepared to respond intentionally following established protocols. The endeavor first involves conducting risk assessments through focus groups, anonymous surveys, and consultation with crisis communication experts to surface vulnerabilities. Compiling insights gathered, leaders can then architect communication strategies, assign responsibilities, run simulations and pressure tests, and create cascade activation procedures that get ahead of brewing situations before they intensify.

When turbulent events ignite out of the blue, the crisis framework provides a guidebook enabling leaders to respond strategically while teams execute coordinated contingency plans. But the system's effectiveness hinges on the leader's mindset long before chaos manifests. Their focused acceptance of inevitable crises, investment in personal resilience, and commitment to understanding risks proves inseparable from the tactical framework itself. United, they form an integrated system positioning organizations to navigate uncertainty.

Facing The Inevitable Storm

Crises remain unavoidable across every industry, often arising without notice and demanding rapid response under relentless scrutiny. Yet among turbulence, opportunities exist for resilient leaders to shine. Executive B distinguished themselves not by wholly preventing a crisis, but by setting themselves apart through focus and preparation beforehand when stakes seemed lower. All leaders will eventually have their resilience tested in the crucible of chaos. Yet crisis-ready leaders who have cultivated resilience and constructed frameworks to activate stand poised to strategically weather the storm rather than be swept away when winds arrive. The choice to prepare begins now, long before thunder rumbles across the skies.

Leading Through Uncertainty

Crises reveal the caliber of an organization's leadership. When volatility strikes, some leaders anchor their teams, swiftly addressing challenges with decisive action to minimize turmoil. Others recoil as chaos unfolds, overwhelmed by complexity and allowing events to intensify through indecisiveness. Most agree: turbulent times often widen performance gaps between organizations as strong leaders distinguish themselves while struggles expose weaker counterparts.

Yet uncertainty remains unavoidable, arriving unannounced and demanding rapid response under intense scrutiny. So how can leaders prepare for the inevitability of chaos? This guide details a 10-step approach to equip executives to respond with agility when winds of change threaten to capsize operations. Mastering these principles distinguishes those who simply react from leaders ready to steer their organization through the most extreme conditions.

Communicate Openly and Often

Silence breeds anxiety for employees and external stakeholders alike when turmoil strikes. Leaders must establish frequent, transparent communication channels to provide perspective on unfolding events. This involves regularly disseminating updates showcasing poise even without complete information. Rather than retreat when lacking answers, leaders should intensify outreach across media formats via email, virtual town halls, and informal video addresses. This consistency demonstrates accountability while combating misinformation.

Leaders can prepare by identifying diverse stakeholder groups, mapping key contacts, and crafting tailored messaging aligned to each audience's interests. When disruption ignites, rapid response protocols engage these channels to minimize ambiguity's corrosive impact. Especially amid complexity, frequent outreach provides ballast.

Catalyze Leadership in Others

Lone rangers falter in times requiring coordinated response across multiple fronts. Rather than limiting leadership to a few decision-makers, organizations must catalyze leadership skills across teams. This empowers mid-level managers to make decisions by distributing authority. As people lead beyond formal titles, innovative solutions emerge close to the action, accelerating adaptation.

To encourage distributed leadership, senior leaders should actively coach emerging talent in units beyond their direct span of control. Intentionally expanding networks deep into the organization builds relationships with future decision-makers before crisis arrives. Simple steps like learning names or hosting skip-level meetings demonstrate commitment to developing others. This cross-pollination pays dividends when disruption necessitates tapping collective leadership capabilities rapidly.

Balance Short-Term and Long-Term Focus

Chaos compels leaders to address immediate tactical needs impacting daily operations. But triage alone risks losing sight of long-term strategy indispensable for lasting success. The tension requires allocating resources to put out fires while preserving vision critical for future prosperity. Rather than fixating on optics when balancing pressing tradeoffs, leaders must honor commitments to strategic programs, even adjusting timelines, to signal priorities.

Navigating these dual mandates first involves identifying the vital few long-term investments unique to the organization's competitive advantage. Leaders should then stress-test budgets, forecasting best and worst case scenarios to prepare for revenue fluctuations. This analysis provides data to inform decisions about asserting short-term flexibility without fully abandoning the future. With clarity of purpose, leaders can make courageous choices amid complexity.

Reinforce Core Values

Turbulence tests corporate identity down to an organization's cultural DNA. Anxiety breeds temptation to abandon ideals that reflect envisioned identity in favor of expediency that trades values for survival. Leaders must anchor teams to mission and amplify founding principles to provide strength when conditions threaten to blow teams off course.

Executives should actively identify and empower employee advocates to embody desired cultural traits from integrity to courage to service. Their visible commitment signals priorities while modeling desired behaviors for others to emulate. Rather than dictating values, leaders should spotlight these culture champions as north stars for navigating uncertainty. This draws power from within even amid external chaos leaders cannot control.

Listen and Engage Empathetically

Stress overload accompanying crises tempts leaders to retreat into isolation when engagement matters most. Great leaders resist insulation, remaining visibly active through town halls, skip-level meetings, and informal conversations. This models openness while gathering insights from the full workforce to inform better decisions. Rather than feigning answers, humility to ask questions counters the hero complex that restricts perspective.

Preparing for this open access means targeting emotional intelligence long before turbulence arrives. Leaders should actively seek feedback about their approachability to identify blindspots early. Sponsoring reverse mentoring programs with younger employees or participating in coaching circles builds self-awareness as well. By confronting fears of vulnerability in calm seasons, leaders stand ready to truly listen rather than retreating when stability fractures.

Expand External Networks

Institutions focused inward rigidify rapidly amid shifting environments demanding adaptation. Great leaders counterbalance internal ties by actively developing diverse external networks to input fresh perspective. Advisory panels, peer roundtables and crisis scenario exercises with other leadership teams build relationships with confidants able to share warnings, opportunities and best practices when volatility disrupts.

This expansive external connectivity must be cultivated long before it is desperately needed in the crucible of crisis. Leaders should devote time connecting with peer executives from adjacent industries, breach echo chambers by following contrary voices, and ask board members to expand access across their spheres of influence. The external view provides context and early warning signs of brewing threats.

Impose Order Amid Information Overload

Early turbulence unleashes information torrents from every direction, producing paralysis by analysis. Great leaders respond rapidly, filtering signals from noise to identify vital interventions. Quickly framing a picture of known priorities and unknown gaps focuses resources on actions within control rather than speculation. Communicating this decisive perspective rallies people starved for direction.

But decisiveness itself relies on leaders' willingness to confront complexity long before volatile events demand immediate choices. Through behaviors like consuming diverse information sources or discussing hypothetical scenarios with mentors, self-aware executives can assess and strengthen their comfort with ambiguity over time. The practice provides readiness to process multifaceted inputs when real-time complexity accelerates.

Demonstrate Decisiveness Around Strategy

Leaders who cling rigidly to past strategic assumptions lose sight of currents shifting beneath them. Great leaders remain unsentimental about tactics that secured past success when environments evolve. They sense when familiar playbooks no longer apply and make courageous choices to adopt new trajectories matching emerging realities.

Executives prepare by becoming avid students of industry transformations past and present across sectors. Deconstructing external case studies of strategic pivots builds acumen to recognize when conditions reach an inflection point. Leaders can further destigmatize course correction by praising team members who challenge assumptions in low-risk contexts. This muscle memory provides confidence to respond deliberately when old strategies falter.

Project Confidence and Realistic Optimism

While leaders must transparently acknowledge harsh realities, radiating fatalism breeds resignation across organizations seeking direction amid uncertainty. Great leaders balance honesty with pragmatic optimism reinforced by their track record. They spotlight organizational strengths proven through past turbulence and map decisive next steps that provide purpose.

This nuanced confidence develops through experiencing smaller crises gradually over time, learning skills to rally people by acknowledging difficulty while reinforcing capability to regain control. Early leadership roles should force young executives out of their comfort zone in manageable ways to build self-assurance. Such exposure enables authentic expressions of empathetic realism leaders draw upon when truly severe crises arise later in their careers.

Model Grit Through Sheer Resilience

Leaders faced with unprecedented adversity experience the same emotional disruption and fatigue that tests organizational endurance. Great leaders master the ability to regulate their own energies, demonstrating extraordinary focus bordering on stoicism regardless of conditions. Their mental toughness lifts collective spirits, with their persistent example giving permission for teams to persevere.

This grit develops only by repeatedly coping firsthand with smaller challenges. Early career tactical roles offer opportunities to build tolerance coping with volatility more directly. Later as executives, self-care routines from nutrition to wellness, along with support structures that enforce rest, enable leaders to sustain composure when calamity extends beyond normal endurance levels. Executives who have pushed past prior perceived limits access confidence in their crisis resilience.

External disruption remains unavoidable, but response separates organizations that nimbly navigate uncertainty from those blown dangerously off course. Crisis reveals the genuinely great leaders worthy of following when stakes intensify. They distinguish themselves long before turbulence emerges by embracing practices and mindsets that position their organization's success when volatility inevitably strikes. Seize the opportunity to prepare before the storm arrives on the horizon - and leave a legacy others wish to follow.

Communication During Crisis

Crisis breeds uncertainty. As volatility unfolds, people seek stability through leaders willing to anchor teams with decisive guidance. Yet turbulent times strain communication channels already overwhelmed by deafening noise. Breaking through the clutter to provide clarity remains vital when visibility plummets. How can executives demonstrate courageous leadership in word and action when markets collapse, social tensions erupt, or pandemics emerge? This guide details battle-tested practices for communicators striving to steer teams through the fog.

What to Communicate: Focus on the Vital Few Messages

Inundated and anxious stakeholders lack bandwidth to process peripheral information. Leaders must identify and highlight essential facts that directly enable response. Start by asking: what specific insights can empower people to act intentionally amid ambiguity? Edit ruthlessly to spotlight critical safety protocols, return-to-work timelines, and support resources as people confront both professional and personal disruption simultaneously. Lead with transparency, acknowledging uncertainties still unfolding while providing regular status updates as new developments emerge.

Rather than defaulting to opaque corporate rhetoric, adopt simpler language acknowledging harsh realities. Leaders modeling humility gain trust while redirecting attention to pockets of stability. Share what remains anchored amid swirling tides like organizational purpose, behavioral values, and service commitments that provide psychological ballast when surface turbulence intensifies. Directly address core questions consuming teams while redirecting fixation on speculation outside their control. Communicate with compassion while inspiring realistic optimism rooted in shared identity.

When to Communicate: Commit to Consistency

One-time announcements easily wash away amid nonstop alerts inundating exhausted audiences. Leaders must establish diverse communication rhythms that repeatedly reinforce priority messages across multiple platforms from email to intranet portals to virtual town halls. Consider launching informal video addresses directly answering pressing concerns. Schedule recurring touchpoints that promise access despite blistering pace of change.

The consistency demonstrates proactive transparency, combating external misinformation that breeds when leaders retreat. People need reassurance their needs have not faded from view as new developments emerge. Setting reliable update cadences, then over-delivering on depth and accessibility builds durable connection. Don't solely rely on official statements - make space for two-way dialogue, acknowledging anxiety and frustration. The exchanges build resilience capacity to weather prolonged turbulence.

How to Communicate: Lead with Empathy

Stress accompanies trauma. People desire human connection amid disruption. Resist hiding behind leadership facades when emotions amplify. Start conversations by checking in on others' well being before diving into tactical agenda. Ask about dominant emotions teams are navigating, normalizing experiences from grief to exhaustion that remain unspoken. Model self-care practices that encourage people to acknowledge their own limits. The compassion for shared struggles builds durable bonds able to withstand extended turmoil.

Listen intently to understand mindsets before attempting to solve problems or placate worries. Ask thoughtful questions drawing out understanding rather than rushing to provide answers yourself. The restraint demonstrates partnership enabling groups to uncover solutions together. Meet face to face virtually to fully gauge reactions when possible. But don't immediately attempt to eliminate tensions. Create space guiding people through various stages of acceptance around adversity. The empathy and understanding lays groundwork for the next stage: Recovery.

Crisis cuts through noise to reveal leaders ready to provide clarity amid chaos versus those who retreat at the moment teams need them most. People desire human connection through the vulnerability, honesty and compassion that anchors organizations threatened by external storms beyond their control. While uncertainty persists, executives able to deliver focused communication with reliability signal purpose helping teams transcend disruption. Their steady hand at the helm can make the difference between those who sink beneath waves of change versus those who sail together to calmer waters. Chart that course with courage and resilience now.

Preparing Teams to Thrive Through Crisis

Crises reveals stark differences between organizations that resiliently bounce back versus those dragged underwater by disruption. Why do some teams emerge stronger while others flounder? Resilience traces back to cultures intentionally built to rapidly adapt when volatility strikes. How can leaders proactively construct organizational resilience to thrive amid unpredictability? This guide details key focus areas to ready teams for turbulence.

Committed Leadership Anchors Resilient Foundations

Resilient cultures start at the top. Employees fixate on leaders' mindsets and actions when uncertainty intensifies. Do executives demonstrate composure? Can they guide teams with decisiveness through complexity? Observing leaders frozen by ambiguity multiplies workforce anxiety exponentially. But confidence from the helm calms nerves. Employees need psychological safety to take risks enabling adaptation. So leaders must first anchor their own resilience to provide ballast across organizations.

Demonstrate personal accountability by directly addressing difficult realities rather than retreating behind bureaucracy's armor. Pursue radical transparency in messaging across channels while inviting two-way dialogue. Launch intranet forums or informal video check-ins to expand access between distributed teams and leadership. Make space for people to voice fears before providing direction. The authenticity builds durable bonds able to withstand prolonged turmoil. Listen then lead.

Strengthen Connective Tissue Through Open Communication

Resilient cultures encourage information flows not just top-down, but cross-functionally. Silos that rigidify communication across units crack under pressure. Stovepipe channels cause mixed messages amplifying confusion when adversity hits. Instead, organizations must adopt common conduits like workplace intranet platforms to centrally coordinate.

Leaders should incentivize knowledge transfer by spotlighting internal subject matter experts willing to hold peer-based masterclasses across business units and geographies. Facilitate self-governed communities of practice to dismantle siloes. The connections tighten meshes able to withstand volatility's fierce impact. Transparency builds trust and shared camaraderie in advance of turbulence.

Prioritize Employee Wellbeing and Balance

Prolonged uncertainty strains personal resilience alongside professional duties. The thin line separating work and life splinters when people juggle escalated workplace expectations alongside family crisis management. Rather than discounting these dueling demands, leaders should encourage authenticity about current stressors. Make space for employees to openly discuss overwhelm without fear of judgement or penalty.

Consider launching dedicated forums allowing people to interact casually with colleagues about shared hobbies and interests. The informal ties provide peer support that enhances resilience capacity when adversity strikes. Promote usage by seeding initial discussion topics then stepping back to let organic communities blossom. The relationships nurture social health and forge bonds able to withstand turmoil.

Embrace Innovation and Accountability

Resilience requires regular adaptation, not just reactionary pivots when backed into corners by disruption. Yet change-averse cultures seeded distrust toward innovation long before crisis emerges make transformation exponentially harder. Leaders seeking continual improvement must first address skepticism by spotlighting technology and process enhancements that saved costs or boosted productivity. The small wins build confidence in change initiatives with longer time horizons.

Further signal commitment by investing in enhanced knowledge management systems like secure cloud-based document repositories with enhanced search functionality. Access to organically updated institutional knowledge helps teams more rapidly respond based on past experience rather than starting from scratch. Leaders should then reinforce usage by directing teams to stored case studies when new challenges arise. Soon people intrinsically tap the knowledge networks as vital tools rather than perceived disruptors.

Unleash the Power of Cross-Functional Teams

Finally, siloed units crumble when impacted by external pressures they cannot address independently. The narrow focus breeds isolation that inhibits enterprise-wide adaptation essential for resilience. To reinforce shared accountability, leaders should launch interdisciplinary "tiger teams" armed with decision authority to tackle challenges. Allow them to organically self-organize based on skillsets and priorities rather than defined hierarchy. Set ambitious key results but resist micromanagement.

Early success by these empowered teams demonstrates the potential of distributed leadership models necessary to navigate uncertainty too complex for top-down response. Provide air cover insulating the groups from bureaucracy while they operate. As wins accumulate, the approach can expand from crisis response units to mainstream business operations. Resilience scales across interconnected groups unified by common purpose.

Crises tests resilience capacity without mercy. But turbulent times represent opportunities for teams to distinguish themselves by demonstrating adaptability enemies of change typically dismiss. Construct cultures centered on engaged leadership, transparent communication, employee empowerment and cross-functional accountability before disruption strikes. Invest now and your organization can emerge from chaos stronger than competitors still trapped fighting yesterday's battles.

Post-Crisis Reflection and Growth

In the aftermath of turbulence, the instinct for weary leaders remains recovery and restoration to reclaim stability lost. Yet the reactive impulse overlooks immense opportunity: crystal clarity of hindsight to prepare for crises yet to come. How can leaders make the most of retrospective clarity? This guide details key steps to learn from turmoil to strengthen teams for the long journey ahead.

Conduct After-Action Reviews

Immediately on the heels of crisis response, emotions and tensions run hot. Still, the moment presents a ripe chance to capture tactical feedback while memories run fresh. Leaders should arrange after-action reviews inviting internal stakeholders and cross-functional partners to directly share their experiences managing volatility on the frontlines.

The facilitated conversations should create space for candid reactions from frustration to pride across units. Discuss scenarios that briefly overwhelmed systems or gaps needing reinforced. Identify contingency plans that accelerated recovery. The insights distill invaluable perspective otherwise dismissed over time as teams regain momentum. Develop action plans to implement improvements or begin adjusting strategies. But remain vigilant against finger pointing that derails future cooperation. Focus on growth.

Incorporate External Perspectives

While internal debriefs provide operational insights from the inside, leaders can gain blindspot-busting perspective by soliciting outside stakeholders directly impacted by fallout. Survey affected customers highlighting areas where communications provided clarity or induced confusion when rapid changes rippled across markets. Interview suppliers about the level of proactivity keeping partners abreast of changing needs. The external lens spotlights assumptions that leadership teams unconsciously bake into crisis response frameworks. Incorporate these invaluable inputs into improvement plans.

Update and Socialize Crisis Management Protocols

Armed with stakeholder feedback, leaders should revisit crisis management plans while the recommendations remain top of mind rather than allowing them to fade behind daily urgencies. Revise infrastructure, technology and communication procedures needing reinforcement in light of new vulnerabilities exposed under stress. Reevaluate and clarify roles for leadership, response teams and partners during escalation scenarios of varying severity. Then pressure test the updated response architecture through simulation scenarios that underscore past blindspots.

Finally, prominently share the revised plans across the organization. Spotlight areas enhanced by stakeholder input to signal responsiveness while underscoring no crisis is ever fully wasted if it prepares teams to outmaneuver the next disruption. Even simply discussing worst case scenarios demystifies the threat reducing risk of freeze responses when calamity strikes again. Proactively socializing protocols organizations the muscle memory needed to react instinctively across units.

Crisis punctuates periods of stability with opportunity to improve resilience for threats ahead. But without structure for intentional reflection, hard-fought experience easily washes away losing its potential to bolster teams for the long road. Leaders play a vital role first creating space for open exchanges in the aftermath, then ensuring conversations convert to enhanced playbooks able to weather the next storm. With each cycle of turbulence, disruption's power diminishes across groups inoculated by continual learning on the road together.

Key Takeaways & Final Thoughts on Crisis Management for Leaders

Key Takeaways:

- Proactive crisis preparation distinguishes resilient leaders ready to act amid ambiguity versus those overwhelmed by complexity

- Robust crisis response requires cultivating crisis-ready mindsets, frameworks and competencies before disruption emerges

- Leaders should intentionally develop external networks, decision-making comfort with uncertainty, communications reflexes and personal resilience

- Empowering leadership across the organization equips more change agents to drive adaptation from the frontlines

- Transparent communication, cross-functional coordination and decentralized authority enable agility when volatility strikes

- Learning must continue after the crisis through intentional reflection to continuously improve resilience

Crisis as a Catalyst for Strength

Crises expose gaps but also reveal potential. Tumultuous times punctuate seasons of stability with opportunity to build organizational resilience for threats ahead. Through the fire, teams either forged stronger or fractured by the flame distinguish themselves. Why? The difference lies in leadership preparation and response long before turbulence strikes.

Resilient leaders accept volatility remains inevitable. Rather than viewing crises as existential threats, they recognize inflection points demanding courageous decisions that ultimately strengthen teams. They invest deeply in crisis competencies from mindset to communication to support structures. They empower others to lead. And they learn relentlessly from turbulence to ratchet organizational resilience ever higher.

In the aftermath, resilient leaders gather insights from stakeholders within and beyond the organization to enhance playbooks. They pressure test updated response plans through simulation. And they transparently share enhanced protocols across all teams, inoculating groups by demystifying disruption's power. With each cycle of chaos turned catalyst, adversity's potential to unravel organizations diminishes across groups unified by shared resilience for the long road together.

The storm will assuredly strike again from new directions. But resilient cultures remain grounded by the timeless question: how can we prepare today to thrive through the next crisis we cannot yet imagine? They respond without hesitation. The future remains uncertain, but readiness should never waver.

Chapter Eleven

Nurturing Innovation and Creativity

Today's leaders face a diverse range of unfamiliar challenges that demand creative solutions. Where stable workflows and predictable outcomes once dominated, uncertainty has become the norm. Effective leaders recognize that yesterday's conventional management strategies are no longer sufficient. Building an adaptable mindset across all levels of an organization is crucial to continued relevance and competitiveness. By prioritizing innovation and cultivating resilience in their workforce, leaders can empower their teams to not only withstand unexpected obstacles but also uncover new opportunities for growth.

The pace and scope of change experienced by many of today's organizations is unprecedented. Remote and hybrid work models mean collaboration dynamics are constantly shifting. Supply chain disruptions create production uncertainties. Consumer behaviors evolve in response to emerging socioeconomic influences. The magnitude of forces in flux makes it difficult to chart a clear path forward. However, through uncertainty lies opportunity. Organizations able to nimbly adapt have a distinct competitive advantage. Their leaders embrace agility, empowering people to think divergently and creatively problem solve in the face of adversity. Rather than recoiling from volatility, the agile leader sees possibility. But adopting an innovation mindset begins with building a resilient workforce.

Forging Resilience by Investing in Human Capital

Resilient employees form the backbone of the agile organization. They demonstrate psychological flexibility when confronting setbacks, rapidly bouncing back and reorienting in dynamic conditions. Resilience arises from human capital investments like skills training, career development opportunities, and organizational support systems. Forward-looking leaders understand that continuously developing talent across all levels of the company safeguards against skills deficiencies that yield vulnerability when disruptions hit. They also foster connectedness and trust between team members, countering the isolation that hampers adaptive capacity. By laying this groundwork during periods of stability, leaders empower employees to handle uncertainty. When disruption inevitably emerges, workers can rely on ingrained capabilities and strong social bonds to persevere. The resulting resilience provides a launch pad for creative solutions.

Sparking Innovation Through Diversity and Inclusion

Resilient employees provide the capacity to endure volatility, while diversity supplies the fuel for transformational thinking. Organizations comprised of professionals with varied backgrounds, skill sets and perspectives unlock innovation potential. By intentionally seeking diversity, leaders gain access to a wealth of experiences and ideas that incite unconventional solutions. To fully capitalize, they must nurture inclusion, encouraging individuals across differences to freely communicate concepts without fear of judgment. Psychologically safe environments activate creativity and critical thinking. People feel emboldened to challenge norms, take risks and learn from failures on the path to innovation. While homogenous teams often reinforce traditional mindsets and status quos, diverse teams breach new ground. The interplay between resilience and diversity forms a springboard to possibility amidst disruption.

The Payoff: Competitive Agility

The business landscape grows more complex each day, but the modern leader must greet uncertainty with opportunity. By prioritizing workforce resilience through human capital investment and psychological safety nets, they lay the groundwork for adaptability. Meanwhile, nurturing diversity and inclusion unlocks the creative potential to confront unfamiliar problems. When volatility emerges, resilient, heterogeneous teams demonstrate agility. They not only endure turbulence but uncover possibilities others overlook, driving competitiveness. Of course, the pace of change will only accelerate, revealing unforeseen obstacles and scenarios. Yet the agile organization, empowered by its people, sees possibility in uncertainty. Their culture of resilience and innovation equips them to consistently evolve ahead of the next disruption, sustaining relevance over the long term. The competitive edge relies not on stability, but on empowering people to shift perspectives and ideate with imagination.

Cultivating a Creative Mindset

Leaders today navigate increasingly complex challenges that demand imaginative solutions. Yet in the push to maintain order amidst uncertainty, many unintentionally suppress their own creative capacities. Despite good intentions, the rigid thinking that stems from perfectionism and risk avoidance often hinders innovation. However, by adopting key mindset shifts and experimental behaviors, leaders can counter convention to unlock dormant creative potential. The path begins with embracing imperfection, finding inspiration in unexpected places, and ultimately transcending limiting perspectives. With an activated creative orientaton, leaders gain the vision to transform obstacles into opportunities.

Escaping the Perfectionist Mindtrap

For many leaders, responsibility fuels an instinct to safeguard order and achieve flawless outcomes. Such perfectionistic thinking builds necessary organizational alignment and accountability when applied judiciously. However, left unchecked, the same tendencies that yield stability can also constrain inventiveness. Leaders devoted to flawlessness begin approaching decisions fearfully, avoiding potential missteps at the expense of fresh concepts. Unconventional ideas face endless scrutiny and revision before seeing the light of day - if they ever do. Soon, teams learn to shelve creative impulses in favor of convention, reinforcing homogeneity. But when disruption inevitably emerges, organizations anchored in tradition find themselves ill-equipped to adapt.

By resisting the illusion of control perfectionism promises, leaders rediscoverlatitude for originality. Progress depends not on identifying the "perfect" solution, but devising one that best fits current needs and abilities. When focused on forward movement rather than precision, missteps transform into learning opportunities rather than failures. Suddenly, brainstorming flourishes and out-of-left-field concepts receive fair consideration. The multiplicity of options then allows analytical selection of the most promising approach. Creativity requires room for imperfection - continuously improving upon iterations matters more than getting it "completely right." Once leaders lift perfectionism's constraints, real innovation becomes attainable.

Seeking Inspiration Through Unconventional Paths

Just as perfectionistic tendencies impede imaginative thinking in leaders, environments stacked towards order and tidiness inadvertently encourage rigidity. Surprisingly, research by Kathleen Vohs of the University of Minnesota reveals messy spaces can provide unexpected catalysts for ingenuity. While cleanliness and organization clearly aid focus and productivity, they also subconsciously prime the mind for convention and risk avoidance. However, entering disarray seems to stimulate non-linear considerations, enhancing receptivity to untested alternatives. The study suggests leaders seeking inspiration loosen the grip on strict structural elements now and then, allowing some ideological clutter to take root.

Beyond tolerating physical messiness, expanding inspirational inputs fuels novelty. Delving into unfamiliar creative arts, hobby explorations, and even simple lifestyle variations provides incremental stepping stones to new perspectives. For example, leaders who view themselves as inartistic can find immense open-mindedness benefits from engaging inner artists through basic drawing or painting. Alternatively, shaking up established weekly routines trains flexibility and pattern interrupting skills transferrable to professional contexts. When the mind grows too accustomed to existing frameworks, inspiration inevitably suffers. By diversifying activities and environments occasionally, leaders prompt refreshed vantage points upon returning to their leadership roles.

Transcending Limitations Through New Perspectives

Ultimately, the obstacles leaders face require solutions found only in uncharted directions. Yet when confronted by unfamiliar disruption and uncertainty, the temptation exists to rigidly cling toConvention. However, reflective leaders realize true adaptation demands more than doubling down on known tactics. Instead, progress comes by embracing restrictiveness as a pathway to greater creativity. Artist Phil Hansen coined the term "embrace the shake" referring to transcendent power that flows from limitations. By accepting setbacks and challenges as spurs for imagination rather than barriers, leaders unlock innovation.

The future promises only increasing complexity, but limitation breeds creation. Therefore, leaders should welcome some messiness, seek inspiration widely, take risks and nurture communities where creativity thrives. The imperfection-embracing mindset builds resilience and ideation skills to turn stumbling blocks into guideposts. Of course, calculated analysis still plays a role to practically scale creative outputs. However, the courage to shake off rigidity and restriction provides raw material to evaluate. Leaders bold enough to regularly step outside their comfort zones gain vision to spot possibilities where others see dead-ends. Thus unblocked, they transform uncertainty from threat into creative advantage.

Cultivating Collaborative Innovation and Trust

For leaders seeking competitive advantage amid complexity, innovation represents an urgent imperative. Pioneering products, disruptive delivery models, transformative customer experiences - breakthroughs arise not from stale convention but creative ingenuity. Yet fostering enterprise-wide innovation transcends installing suggestion boxes or scheduling brainstorming sessions. True cultural transformation requires laying psychological and interpersonal foundations so creativity emerges organically at all levels.

By establishing environments where people feel safe to experiment and empowered to collaborate, leaders spur innovation organically. Trust constitutes a cornerstone - freedom from fear enables bold ideation. Furthermore, community catalyzes creativity via diversity and inclusion; bringing varied perspectives together into psychologically-safe teams unlocks potential. Of course toxic individuals can undermine efforts, stifling imagination through judgment. However, leaders investing relationship capital position organizations to collectively spark breakthroughs. People feeling valued and heard freely contribute ideas, combining complementary strengths for multidimensional solutions. The collaborative interplay therefore becomes greater than isolated efforts - inclusion empowers.

Securing Foundations of Trust

To channel human potential toward creative problem solving, leaders must first cultivate environments where employees feel confident exploring and testing new concepts freely. People anxious about reproach for imperfect ideas default to convention, playing it safe rather than voicing bold new directions. Leaders can establish safe creative spaces by upholding fairness, inviting input across all levels on decisions affecting employees. Seeking wide ranging perspectives communicates respect and concern for people's preferences, building loyalty and engagement.

Essentially this interpersonal dynamic comes down to trust. Leaders serious about sparking innovation must demonstrate genuine care for employees' development and wellbeing. Even small acts acknowledging individuals' contributions make them feel valued within community. In turn, feeling personally secure and invested in organizational success focuses talent inward. People give their best ideas to cultures recognizing their best selves. Every leader must self-reflect on tone, transparency and compassion dynamics that foster the trust to inspire team members' discretionary effort.

Clearing Toxic Forces That Contaminate Community

In parallel, leaders must act decisively to eliminate toxic individuals exhibiting behaviors that corrode collaborative creativity from the inside out. Regardless of historical performance or connections, hostile employees inflict psychological violence eroding creative capacity enterprise-wide. Through subtle criticism and dismissal of unconventional concepts, they shame newcomers into conformity and self-censoring. Even a few toxic personalities undermine majority goodwill efforts by leaving employees hesitant to engage openly.

Therefore, leaders must establish and uphold behavioral standards aligned to psychological safety so all feel welcome contributing. When toxic patterns emerge, quick correction communicating expected mutual respect is essential. However, some individuals remain corrosive forces despite feedback. Though never easy, cutting ties frees resources for new team members to fill capability gaps. This further communicates everyone is accountable to cultural values at all levels, renewing community commitment. Overall its far better to have a vacancy than toxicity contaminating collaboration, creativity and trust.

Catalyzing Creativity Through Inclusive Communities

For organizations to tap full creative capacity, trust provides the safety net while diversity supplies the spark. Leaders bringing together cross-functional teams with multifaceted skill sets, backgrounds and world views gain access to a wealth of experiential knowledge to inspire innovation ideation. The interactive exchange of varying thought patterns, mental models and emotional intelligence often unveils unforeseen connections and possibilities.

However, capitalizing on these differentiated perspectives requires inclusion - leveraging diversity is impossible without equitable voice and protection against judgment. Though counterintuitive in hierarchical structures, the leader's role becomes more horizontal - less singular vision authority, more facilitator enabling all contributors. This empowers ideas to surface freely, subject to collaborative examination rather than individual pre-vetting. Embracing radical candor over toxicity helps refine notions constructively, rather than shaming as ego protection. Soon, people expand on one another's suggestions to uncover unconventional solutions together, combining complementary strengths for multidimensional breakthroughs.

Thus diversity and inclusion interdependence grows organization-wide creative capacity exponentially. Too often leaders paralyze innovation by centralizing control rather than distributing authority to where information and insight reside. Those closest to operations best understand domain challenges and consumer pain points prime for disruptive solutions. Trusted and empowered, they collaboratively unlock game changing ideas through uninhibited creativity.

The Path Forward

Innovation springs not from cubes but culture - the contexts leaders cultivate unconsciously shape strategic outcomes. Dictatorial environments fertilize fearfulness choking creativity before fruits ripen. However, psychologically safe cultures flowering trust and respect bear harvests of unconventional concepts and breakthrough results.

Of course ideas require refinement into value generating implementation, hence leaders maintain essential strategy guiding roles. However, source material originates across all levels - often unseen pockets closest to the problem. Therefore wise leaders seek diversity, demonstrate compassion and nurture talent. With foundations of trust established, they empower community creativity to rise collectively. Though disruption always looms, inclusive organizations stay agile - facing the unknown future together.

Overcoming Barriers to Creativity

Developing breakthrough solutions to complex problems ultimately requires imagination and ingenuity. While leaders often consider creativity the exclusive domain of R&D teams or marketing units, the capacity for innovation resides within every employee. However, even individuals brimming with ideas often self-censor, as implicit fears manifest into barriers throttling creative expression. By recognizing imagination as a multidimensional journey, leaders can take targeted action to dismantle roadblocks at each step of the creative process. Establishing psychologically safe environments where people acknowledge fears liberates latent creative capacities across entire organizations.

The Spark of Imagination: Widening Experiential Repertoires

The genesis of novel concepts relies on accumulation of diverse experiences to draw from. Individuals exposed to varied disciplines, challenges and worldviews assemble richer mental mosaic pieces reflecting broader perspectives. This experiential repertoire then fuels associations between seemingly disconnected notions other minds overlook. However, many hesitant to violate standards or exit comfort zones consciously avoid unfamiliar encounters. Risk aversion then stagnates imagination as comfort of convention outweighs exploring the foreign.

Leaders play pivotal roles empowering people to multiply experiences by embracing unfamiliarity. Explicit encouragement to pursue progress over perfection helps teams reframe missteps as learning opportunities rather than failures. Incremental forays into adjacent domains stretch perspectives just enough while building confidence to try again. Leaders equally growth focused on capability expansion versus short term gains signal purpose over outcomes, inspiring engagement. Soon curiosity overrides caution, as ideas sparked by new exposures kindle innovative connections. Still, lingering doubts require support to translate imagination into impactful solutions.

Channeling Creativity: Making Meaningful Associations

While fresh experiences may ignite initial sparks, synthesizing creative connections demands blending concepts and contexts to uncover possibility. This associative capacity often occurs unconsciously through sudden "eureka" moments manifesting ingenious solutions. Other innovations emerge by deliberately comparing ideas previously viewed as unrelated, revealing interplays only visible from certain angles. Unfortunately rational traditions that prioritize logic undermine the organic meandering central to combinatory creativity. Quick to dismiss unstructured rumination as inefficient, pragmatists often rush to analytical conclusion at the expense of illumination.

Leaders seeking to nurture associative abilities must first legitimize creativity's messy phases as essential waypoints in problem solving journeys rather than aimless wandering. Reserving space for self-dialogue and reflection provides firmer foundations when aligning disparate notions into unified frameworks later. Patience for indeterminate processing also pays dividends - the subconscious synthesizes concepts even absent direct attention. Trusting outcomes to manifest in due course rather than forcing immediate conclusions liberates breakthrough thinking. Of course leaders still ensure teams converge imaginative outputs into targeted solutions, providing project parameters to bound brainstorming. However, by first opening minds to possibility without preconception, ingenious associations unlock potential hiding in plain sight.

Voicing Ideas: Overcoming Expressive Hesitancy

While awakened imagination and channeled creativity generate promising possibilities internally, leaders need strategies to help individuals voice embryonic notions aloud. Despite holding solutions in mind, many hesitate sharing half-formed concepts fearing harsh judgment or rejection before fully formulated. Unasserted ideas then never capture complementary contributions from colleagues that may evolve notions toward Excellence. Breaking this cycle requires establishing environments where people feel psychologically safe to think freely without self-censoring.

Leaders play central roles modeling receptive engagement that affirms rather than admonishes new ideas openly. Radical candor that unpacks contributions in constructive fashion builds confidence to venture imperfect suggestions, embracing iteration. Furthermore, framing creativity as a collective community endeavor alleviates pressure on sole originators to present polished proposals ready for immediate execution.instead, collaborative co-creation provides support to translate insights into viable deliverables. Of course leaders still filter options based on experience, but leaving space for unconventional concepts keeps innovation pipelines flowing freely. Soon, employees recognize their insights contribute to progress in some form.

Discerning Ideas: Evaluative Empathy for Embryonic Notions

After encouraging expression, leaders must hone evaluative skills that distinguish transformational ideas from ineffective ones. However, rather than relying on traditional metrics, assessment requires context and empathy. Novel proposals often appear underdeveloped or impractical initially when holding future facing promise. Quick dismissal risks losing breakthroughs simply needing nurturing and modification to blossom. On the other hand, misguided concepts waste resources and distract focus if allowed to linger too long. Therefore leaders balance openness for unorthodox proposals with prudent decision making.

Here psychological safety again plays a pivotal role by decoupling self-worth judgments from ideation, allowing constructive refinement. Leaders make clear that options have inherent merits, while strategy dictations and feasibility filters choices. This maintains contributors' dignity and engagement despite concept disruption. Wise leaders also recognize evaluation skills develop overtime through exposure versus instant mastery. Modeling humble learning attitudes helps teams iterate ideas together without ego interfering. Ultimately solutions reach viability through extensive shaping. Thus leaders concentrate on progress enabled by imagination's outputs rather than demanding instant perfection.

Realizing Innovation: Cultivating Tenacity and Reward

Finally, catalyzing creativity requires fueling perseverance to carry unconventional ideas through resistance and setbacks bound to emerge with disruption. On pathways less travelled, determination supersedes skill in achieving breakthroughs. Yet self-doubt plagues innovation pioneers unable to foresee desired ends clearly. Leaders therefore equip teams for the long haul by celebrating small early wins that build momentum. When individuals experience payoffs from initial creative risks, confidence in capacities grows. Momentum then provides resilience to weather later obstacles.

Additionally, leaders seeking cultural transformation demonstrate commitment by integrating imagination into company values and rewards systems. Compensation and performance metrics tied directly to creative contributions signal priority beyond slogans. Even modest rewards recognizing unconventional initiatives cultivate the conviction needed to see episodic ideas to fruition. Soon passionate pioneers spread courageous creativity through teams by example. Despite inevitable barriers, mutually reinforcing perseverance transforms employee creativity from occurrence into organizational competency.

By acknowledging imagination requires an iterative journey, leaders pinpoint specific developmental milestones to facilitate. Incremental exposure, divergent thinking, voice activation, evaluative empathy and resolute resilience together unlock dormant creative potential at cultural scale. The nonlinear process honors creativity's emergent nature while providing supportive guardrails to reach solutions. With barriers removed, creative capacities thrive, driving innovation even amidst disruption's uncertainty.

Key Takeaways & Final Thoughts on Nurturing Innovation and Creativity

Key Takeaways:

- Leaders can catalyze creativity by resisting perfectionism and establishing psychologically safe environments where people feel comfortable sharing embryonic ideas

- Eliminating toxic forces that undermine trust and psychological safety is essential, even when difficult, to enable collaborative creativity

- Diversity provides raw materials for creativity but inclusion through equitable voice and constructive development of ideas is vital to fully leverage these perspectives

- Recognizing barriers at each phase of the creative process allows targeted interventions to nurture imagination into innovations

Cultivating an Innovative Culture

In an increasingly complex business landscape, reliance on past strategies spells peril, making creativity-fueled innovation an urgent imperative. Yet inspiring enterprise-wide creativity requires more than brainstorming sessions or suggestion boxes. True cultural transformation demands establishing fertile contexts where creative capacities bloom across entire organizations.

By resisting perfectionistic constraints, encouraging small risks, and fostering trust through transparency, leaders prompt people to think expansively, unlocking the imagination that sparks breakthrough concepts. Psychologically safe environments then empower employees to develop embryonic ideas collaboratively without fear of harsh judgments. Diversity provides adjacencies forging unconventional connections, while inclusion gives space for notions to refine towards excellence. Even creativity's barriers transform into catalysts when met with empathy and tenacious support. Soon passionate pioneers permeate teams, normalizing imagination's outputs into innovative outcomes.

Of course, complexity confounds forecasts, ensuring disruption always lurks unseen over the horizon. Yet turbulence breeds opportunity for leaders bold enough to resist rigidity and embrace agility. With foundations of trust established and barriers transformed into launchpads, creative cultures synthesized across functions and roles gain vision to spot unseen possibilities. Unfettered imaginations then uncover solutions where others see only dead-ends. Ultimately creativity manifests not in processes, but psychologically safe people unified by vision-led values. By nurturing imagination's multidimensional journey from spark to implementation, leaders transform uncertainty from threat into sustainable competitive advantage.

The future belongs to the creative. However, establishing creative competence requires cultural commitment - not just indulging innovation theatrics. How will you foster trust and inclusion enterprise-wide to empower rising ideas? What small risks today unlock big breakthroughs tomorrow? With foundations set, where will you guide your people's imaginations toward next?

Chapter Twelve

Conclusion: Your Personal Voyage

Leadership presents a lifelong voyage filled with rocky waters and sunlit horizons ahead for those ready to chart their course. While theories, frameworks and competencies provide helpful navigational tools, ultimately you must captain your own ship. Defining true north requires looking within first - clarifying the purpose propelling you forward through mounting waves or languid doldrums alike. What legacy will you leave in your wake - both personal and professional?

With so many divergent perspectives on leadership flooding the discourse, determining appropriate models feels akin to assembling a puzzle with pieces plucked randomly across decades and contexts. However, common threads emerge around the significance of self-awareness, adaptability, ethical grounding and nurturing talent in others. The route you chart relies on continually realigning these elements as landscapes and organizations evolve.

Fundamentally, leadership forms an inward journey before manifesting externally through actions big and small. Establishing solid foundations requires addressing fears, false narratives and insecurities that restrict authenticity. Mustering courage to stand firmly yet compassionately for personal truths and shared values lays pavement enabling forward movement.

Meanwhile, the terrain itself morphs continuously - economically, politically, technologically and generationally. Chartering unknown waters demands flexibility in reinventing skill sets, mindsets and communication styles to resonate across stakeholders. Leaders attuned to seismic undercurrents intentionally upskill into emerging competencies primed for contemporary challenges.

However, chasing after each passing fad rings hollow without an ethical compass providing orientation. True north relies not on rules, controls or incentives but rather integrity ingrained into every molecule. Leadership credibility necessitates embodying espoused virtues within organizational cultures through transparency, empowerment and caring.

The enterprise must also outlive any single leader's tenure. Establishing robust succession plans distributes wisdom across rising generations. Beyond knowledge transfer lies a deeper legacy - imprinting timeless values through mentoring. Such cultivation requires igniting potential already simmering inside rather than imposing expectations externally. Release fixations with molding protégés into mini replicas; instead empower diverse thinkers and doers to chart new paths while avoiding previous pitfalls.

Ultimately these voyages last beyond single careers or lifetimes - leadership lives on through talent developed, cultures transformed and communities impacted. While formal authority offers a transitory vehicle for influence, inspiration sparks relay races transporting vision across decades. Understanding this broader context and contribution helps leaders progress from grasping tightly onto temporary power towards empowering endless ripples.

What emerges is a continually evolving dance between iterating technical expertise, credibility rooted in ethical grounding and focus toward unlocking human potential. Master the basics, align to your truth north and then get out of your own way to allow brilliance in others space to manifest. Bon voyage, leader - now chart your course!

www.ingramcontent.com/pod-product-compliance
Lightning Source LLC
Chambersburg PA
CBHW060052260726
48658CB00004B/1275